The Rational Guide To

IT Project
Management

D1416030

PUBLISHED BY

Rational Press - An imprint of the Mann Publishing Group
208 Post Road, Suite 102
Greenland, NH 03840, USA
www.rationalpress.com
www.mannpublishing.com
+1 (603) 601-0325

ISBN: 1-932577-17-3
Library of Congress Control Number (LCCN): 2004115496
Printed and bound in the United States of America.
10 9 8 7 6 5 4 3 2 1

Trademarks

Mann Publishing, Mann Publishing Group, Agility Press, Rational Press, Inc.Press, NetImpress, Farmhouse Press, BookMann Press, The Rational Guide To, Rational Guides, ExecuGuide, AdminExpert, From the Source, the Mann Publishing Group logo, the Agility Press logo, the Rational Press logo, the Inc.Press logo, Timely Business Books, Rational Guides for a Fast-Paced World, and Custom Corporate Publications are all trademarks or registered trademarks of Mann Publishing Incorporated.

All brand names, product names, and technologies presented in this book are trademarks or registered trademarks of their respective holders.

Disclaimer of Warranty

While the publisher and author(s) have taken care to ensure accuracy of the contents of this book, they make no representation or warranties with respect to the accuracy or completeness of the contents of this book and specifically disclaim any implied warranties or merchantability or fitness for a specific purpose. The advice, strategies, or steps contained herein may not be suitable for your situation. You should consult with a professional where appropriate before utilizing the advice, strategies, or steps contained herein. Neither the publisher nor author(s) shall be liable for any loss of profit or any other commercial damages, including but not limited to special, incidental, consequential, or other damages.

Credits

Author:	Jeremy Kadlec
Technical Editor:	Greg Robidoux
Copy Editor:	Jeff Edman
Book Layout:	Molly Barnaby
Series Concept:	Anthony T. Mann
Cover Concept:	Marcelo Paiva

All Mann Publishing Group books may be purchased at bulk discounts.

The Rational Guide To

IT Project Management

Jeremy Kadlec

RATIONAL PRESS

An imprint of the
www.mannpublishing.com

About the Author

Jeremy Kadlec serves as the Principal Database Engineer at Edgewood Solutions (www.edgewoodsolutions.com), a technology services company delivering full spectrum Microsoft SQL Server Services in North America. He has been building technical solutions primarily focused on large-scale SQL Server™ 6.5, 7.0 and 2000 platforms with business critical mid to large sized databases. Further, he has set and implemented a number of SQL Server standards to include Upgrades to SQL Server 2000, EMC Migrations, Application Development, Unattended Installations, Hardware/Software Configurations, Disaster Recovery, Database Security, Server Maintenance and System Performance Tuning. Jeremy has been able to implement these solutions as a technical Project Manager and Lead DBA by standardizing a project management methodology which can be used across projects and passed on to new team members.

Jeremy is also a regular public speaker, having spoken at SQL PASS, local events, and at organizations on a variety of pertinent IT topics. In addition, he has authored numerous articles that have been published on www.SearchDatabase.com, www.SSWUG.org, www.SQL-Server-Performance.com and www.SQLServerCentral.com. He also publishes white papers on various SQL Server topics and serves as an "Ask the Expert" at www.SearchDatabase.com. Jeremy holds a Master's Degree in Information Systems from the University of Maryland, Baltimore County.

Mr. Kadlec is available for Project Management engagements, seminars and workshops for organizations of all sizes. Based on your needs, a customized session can be delivered to benefit you, your department, and your entire organization. Feel free to contact Jeremy at 410.591.4683 or jeremyk@edgewoodsolutions.com.

Dedication

To Kris for all of your love, encouragement and long hours to help make this a reality...

To all of my family for their love and major impacts in my life, especially my Mom and Dad, Baba and Dido, Baba and Gramps, Jessie, Katie, Uncle Rich, Mama Dennis...

To the entire Edgewood Team, especially Greg, Craig, Larry and Sheryl...

To entire Mann Publishing Team for this opportunity and numerous recommendations for a professional publication...

To Robert, Greg, and David for beneficial recommendations for this publication...

To countless friends I have had the distinct pleasure to work with during my career...

To all of the readers, enjoy!

Rational Guides for a
Fast-Paced World™

About Rational Guides

Rational Guides, from Rational Press, provide a no-nonsense approach to publishing based on both a practicality and price that make them rational. Rational Guides are compact books of fewer than 200 pages. Each Rational Guide is constructed with the highest quality writing and production materials — at a price of US$19.99 or less. All Rational Guides are intended to be as complete as possible within the 200-page size constraint. Furthermore, all Rational Guides come with bonus materials, such as additional chapters, applications, code, utilities, or other resources. To download these materials, just register your book at www.rationalpress.com. See the instruction page at the end of this book to find out how to register your book.

Who Should Read This Book

This book is intended for both IT Professionals new to Project Management and experienced Project Managers. Newbies will benefit from the extensive workflow processes and templates. For the seasoned professionals, I am sure the stories will sound familiar, but you will have some new techniques to add to your tool chest for upcoming projects.

Introduction

"What you do speaks so loudly that I cannot hear what you say."
—Ralph Waldo Emerson

Do you feel like you are spinning your wheels while trying to tackle Information Technology (IT) projects? At the same time, do you know that you are not completing important projects that are of great interest to you? Have you thought about what is causing this stress and unsatisfying productivity at work?

These are typical problems that IT Professionals face on a daily basis. So what is to blame for this loss of time, dissatisfaction and gray hair? I believe it is the lack of IT Professionals with project management and technical skills who can define, organize, document, communicate and manage the implementation of a successful solution with a cohesive team.

In this book, I want to share my project management experiences that have led me to the numerous recommendations I have outlined. I began managing IT projects as most IT Project Managers begin, based on necessity rather than a conscious decision to become a Project Manager. I started managing projects at two organizations and have expanded ever since. Neither organization had Project Management practices in place. Both companies had mid to large-scale IT infrastructures and numerous projects with impending deadlines. In both circumstances, the projects impacted my job and were beneficial to the company. These opportunities allowed me to continuously develop my technical skills, which I enjoy to this day, while also beginning to build and fine tune a new skill set called Project Management.

At the first organization, the Y2K problem was at the forefront because of the hype in the media and the looming fear of malicious lawsuits. The entire company was aware of the Y2K problem and recognized the impact, but no one from the IT Department was willing to identify, coordinate and address the issues as a comprehensive project. Since I was new to the company, I wanted to observe how the more seasoned Developers would address the issues. As time passed and pressure mounted, I stepped up to the plate, with encouragement from a particular IT Executive, and with my prior Project Lead experience from smaller development and infrastructure projects. This was at a time when no one else in the organization had much interest in addressing these needs.

This was my first large-scale project in which the entire IT Department, and individuals from the business units, participated in a project under my direction. Luckily, this project was a success and I was recommended to lead SQL Server Upgrade projects for the core business systems at this organization. During this project, I continued to fine tune a new skill set that has benefited me ever since.

During the start-up ".com" rage, I managed both business and IT initiatives that exposed me to new aspects of Project Management. When the bubble burst, I began providing solutions for another organization with numerous SQL Servers that needed improvements and upgrades throughout the United States. At this organization, I took my Project Management skills to the next level. I was charged with building a standardized project methodology that would allow me to provide a full-scale technical and project management solution. I like to call this the "divide and conquer" approach, which can be leveraged by the entire team. As more projects of similar magnitude needed to be addressed, I continued to use the same approach to build the solution and then "divide and conquer" among the team. This approach has been beneficial!

I have since had the opportunity to work on both infrastructure and application development projects where the end goal, team and technology were different, but the process remained the same. Whether you are working on security implementations, storage management, integration, eBusiness or mobile computing, or whether you are in the Finance, Health Care, Government or the High Tech industry, the process and recommendations in this book will benefit you for your future projects.

I have come to realize that Project Management is a significant issue and a vital need for organizations. Appreciating this need, I decided some time ago that I wanted to contribute to the IT field by specializing in Project Management. Once I made this decision, I took the time to mentally walk through all the projects I have ever worked on, outlining the pros and cons, as well as everything I learned from each project. This work yielded a Project Management presentation that I delivered at the SQL PASS 2002 Community Summit in Seattle, Washington.

Since then, I have delivered the presentation in the Metropolitan Washington DC area on a number of occasions. The comments, questions and concerns I have received from these presentations and my experiences have led to this book.

My goal is to provide a practical and standardized project methodology that is not technology-specific. This publication is intended to serve as an iterative guide to Project Management that can be read one chapter at a time to gain insight. Each chapter is intended to benefit the reader by providing recommendations to effectively run a project. This methodology focuses on efficiency and quality, to maximize both your time as an employee and the profits that your organization derives from your contributions. As an IT Professional, you will recognize that Project Management is a cornerstone of the industry. Adopting the methodology in this book for your current and future projects will help you to serve as an asset to both the IT Department and to the entire organization.

Conventions Used In This Book

The following conventions are used throughout this book:

▶ *Italics* — First introduction of a term.

▶ **Bold** — Exact name of an item or object that appears on the computer screen, such as menus, buttons, dropdown lists, or links.

▶ `Mono-spaced text` — Used to show a Web URL address, computer language code, or expressions as you must exactly type them.

▶ **Menu1⇨Menu2** — Hierarchical Windows menus in the order you must select them.

Tech Tip:
This box gives you additional technical advice about the option, procedure, or step being explained in the chapter.

Note:
This box gives you additional information to keep in mind as you read.

 Bonus:
This box lists additional free materials or content available on the Web after you register your book at `www.rationalpress.com`.

Caution
This box alerts you to special considerations or additional advice.

Contents

Contents

Contents

Contents

Planning the Project

Chapter 1

Getting Started With IT Project Management

"The two most important requirements for major success are: first, being in the right place at the right time, and second, doing something about it."
—Ray Kroc

What is an IT Project? An IT project is the combination of People, Processes and Technology to meet an organizational need. Projects are geared toward solving a business problem or improving the efficiency of the organization to save time and money. In this sense, IT is a means by which revenue can be generated or efficiencies can be improved. Currently, life in IT is such that you need to "do more with less." The challenge for everyone in an organization is to perform efficiently in the same time frame and with the same quality.

What is IT Project Management? IT Project Management is a process consisting of the following logical steps for the Project Manager and team:

▶ Define

▶ Organize

▶ Document

▶ Communicate

▶ Manage

These logical steps apply to each project phase and even to particular tasks. For example, it is no good to go into a Status Meeting and discuss irrelevant items in a random manner. This would waste everyone's time. If you have a meeting and do not document the meeting minutes, this information will not be available for future use. Losing this information can result in a difficult decision-making process for the remainder of the project. You need to define, organize, document, communicate and manage the meeting in order to achieve the goal associated with conducting the meeting.

Furthermore, the IT Project Management process is combined with People and Technology. It is necessary to have the appropriate people and technology to make a project successful. A successful project can be calculated as follows:

Successful Project = People + Process + Technology

As IT Professionals, we can all implement the latest and greatest technology, correct? We are able to churn out code and build cool interfaces, right? The problem we run into is working with other individuals in different departments in our organizations. The root cause of this problem is typically communication. Because this problem is so critical and prevalent, a Communications Plan is necessary to address common communication items in proper order, and to interact more efficiently for the benefit of the entire project.

Project Management Business Need

As IT Projects become more complex due to changing business requirements, and the time to implement projects dwindles before a looming deadline, it is difficult, if not impossible, to implement the needed technical solutions without standardized Project Management. A practical and standardized process can mitigate risk whether the project is for SQL Server Upgrades, Infrastructure Implementations or Development Projects. It is possible to address not only difficult technical issues, but also technical-logistics issues by focusing on the project in terms of People, Processes and Technology, yielding a successful project.

It is first necessary to understand the phases of the project and goals for each phase. Next, you must leverage key Project Documents which can be re-used for future projects. The final key to Project Management is the Communication

Plan. With these three components and a realization that success revolves around People, Processes and Technology, successful projects can be implemented on-time and on-budget to positively benefit organizations.

Current Project Management Problems

One of the most common questions I have been asked is: "Why is it so difficult to complete an IT project correctly?" Unfortunately, on-time and on-budget projects that meet business needs are rare. Projects typically become costly to businesses as scope, competition and customer demands increase. One eye-opening statistic from the Standish Group's Chaos Studies is that the success rates for projects at large organizations that are completed on time and within budget are a staggering 9%, with only 42% of the functionality delivered.

Although I believe no single reason can be attributed to these project failure rates, I have observed the following items that I believe contribute to overall Project failure:

▶ *Practical Project Management is not well understood*, and has been viewed as theoretical or "touchy feely," rather than as a repeatable process for technical staff to follow for IT Projects.

▶ *Projects are typically addressed in a "silo" scenario versus a comprehensive solution.* When Developers are notified about a project, they build an ASP page; as DBAs hear about the project, they write a stored procedure; Network Engineers prepare a server. A comprehensive solution needs the collaboration of multiple groups. It is less efficient to have these individuals build components independently and then hope that things work out properly. As Abraham H. Maslow said, "When the only tool you own is a hammer, every problem begins to resemble a nail."

▶ *Project Management is typically not taught* in Information Systems or Computer Science classes, but IT Professionals are expected to lead, manage and participate in projects with multiple team members in order to benefit the organization.

▶ *Typically, Project Management is not interesting to technical staff.* Many individuals are only interested in working with the latest and greatest technology in an ad hoc fashion.

▶ *Project Management is not seen as valuable in some organizations.* Many think it is easier to work quickly through the issues, which seems to take less time than actually planning the project. Too often, a technology can be implemented for its own sake in the short term, but at the cost to the organization of not resolving the true long-term business problem at hand. Furthermore, ongoing maintenance costs and bug fixes are far more expensive than if the time was taken to plan and execute a well thought-out solution at the start of the initiative.

▶ *An ideal Project Manager requires IT experience related to the project, Personnel Management skills and Organizational Skills,* in order to deliver a complete project solution. Unfortunately, it is difficult to recruit and hire individuals in the marketplace that meet these criteria.

▶ *IT staff is overburdened with numerous projects and operates like a firefighter when resolving business problems.* It is often difficult to make this paradigm shift. Unfortunately, by not dedicating time to mature the IT processes, it will be difficult to ever stop working in a reactive rather than a proactive mode.

▶ *Technical Projects are not well-defined.* As business needs shift, poorly-defined projects are hard to complete. By properly determining the project boundaries and goals, it will become easier to better align the projects with business needs and to calculate an accurate return for the project.

▶ *Communication is a key Project Management skill that does not come naturally to many IT staffers.* Communication has as much value as one's technical expertise from years of working in the industry. To achieve professional success, it is necessary to develop communication skills in the same way that technical skills continue to be developed.

The remainder of the book will elaborate on strategies to address each of these items. Unfortunately, all of these items cannot be addressed for all Project Managers 100% of the time. I hope this information will prove beneficial to you in future Project Management opportunities.

Project Management Example: SQL Server 2000 Upgrade

To elaborate on Project Management techniques, this book will leverage an example of a SQL Server 6.5 to 2000 Upgrade. This project was selected because upgrades are a typical project that most IT Professionals have worked through at some time during their careers, although any web development or infrastructure project could have been used instead. For this Upgrade example, the project staff will include Stakeholders, Users, Network Administrators, Desktop Technicians, Testers, Developers and Database Administrators – all of whom are critical to a project's success. Since the focus is Project Management, the Upgrade technical details will be minimal, but the Project Management information will be plentiful.

The following high-level Project Management topics will be addressed:

► Project Management Overview

► Project Management Life Cycle

► Project Break Down Strategy

► Key Project Documents

► Communication Plan

► Risk Mitigation

► Team Personnel Recommendations

► Project Management Templates

Lessons Learned

▶ Project Management is a process that generally follows the following steps: Define, Organize, Document, Communicate and Manage.

▶ Successful projects are bound to People, Processes and Technology.

▶ IT Project Management is a key IT and Business need, vital to the success of the organization and its goals.

▶ As Project Management failures increase at organizations, it is necessary to identify and understand the problems in order to make proper corrections.

Chapter 2

Project Management in a Nutshell

"Rank does not confer privilege or give power. It imposes responsibility."
- Peter F. Drucker

Depending on the organization, the location of the Project Managers in the organizational chart differs. Project Management could be a stand-alone department outside of IT, or a department within IT, or even incorporated into Operational, Engineering and Development groups. Nevertheless, numerous skills are required for an ideal Project Manager.

IT Professionals are great technicians, but typically would benefit from improvements in planning, communication and documentation. These skills, in conjunction with a solidified process, can yield a top-notch Project Manager capable of successfully implementing solutions. Table 2.1 outlines a number of strengths that I believe Project Managers can bring to the project.

One major item derived from Table 2.1 is accountability. Accountability starts with the Project Manager, and leading by example cannot be overlooked. The Project Manager's example serves as a framework for the remainder of the team to follow. Accountability is critical for the team members and for the organization. We will discuss this in more detail in Chapter 5.

ID	Skill	Description
1	Leadership	Recognized and respected by team members by the ability to influence individuals internal and external to the project and rally the team to achieve the project goals
2	Integrity	Personal, project and team honesty in all interactions and situations
3	Planning	Goal-oriented approach to Project Management with a focus on setting goals and a passion to exceed these goals while meeting all project deadlines
4	Technology Experience	Familiarity with the existing and emerging technologies to provide value for the project to make the appropriate technical decisions
5	Analysis	Ability to determine a problem, generate options to resolve the problem and select the most appropriate option to resolve the problem Detail- oriented approach to ensure no major or minor issues surface that negatively impact the project
6	Mediation	Ability to respect the differences of opinion among team members, assemble the team to resolve the dispute and finalize consensus as a resolution
7	Communicaton	Deliver valuable information both verbally and in writing at the appropriate level for the audience via numerous mediums
8	Organization	Organize all communications, documentation and expectations to minimize miscommunications or inefficiencies among the team
9	Determination	Non-stop attitude to work through adversities and accurately complete the project
10	Quality	Focus on quality that permeates all aspects of the project with the foresight in the early stages of the project to build a reliable, maintainable and scalable solution Work towards little to no re-work, by emphasizing accuracy on the first delivery

Table 2.1: Project Manager Skills.

Project Life Cycle

By most accounts, Project Management originated in the construction industry where it was necessary to precisely coordinate resources for building roadways and bridges. When Project Management was adopted in the IT field, it was originally applied to the Systems Development Life Cycle (SDLC). The SDLC was developed with a systematic process in mind — to start with the project requirements and end with the completed system. The SDLC is also referred to as the "Water Fall" model because of its linear process. It is most frequently leveraged on Government projects where the current phase must be completed in order to proceed to the next phase of the project.

More recently, the Rapid Application Development (RAD) Methodology was developed to serve as more of an iterative approach to systems development with frequent user interactions. The RAD approach is used mainly on private sector projects where the core functionality is developed as a prototype and then additional modules are added to complete the project.

I am suggesting a hybrid of these widely accepted software development methodologies. In addition, I suggest formalizing particular steps in the project that are often overlooked, such as the Project Scope, Kick-Off and Lessons Learned. I believe these steps provide valuable direction for the project. I suggest starting with the Project Scope. This is where the Executive buy-in for the need of the project is achieved. I must stress the importance of gaining team member trust at this level. It is important to have their support through the project bumps and bad times. The Project Scope is followed by a detailed Requirements Analysis for the entire project, which outlines iterative Design, Development and Testing phases, starting with a pilot and then proceeding to additional modules. Next, the technical staff completes an iterative series of Design, Development and Preliminary Testing. As modules are finished, Formalized Testing is completed with accompanying corrections. When User Training and Documentation are finalized, the system will be implemented as a pilot. In order to complete the next phase, it is necessary to return to the Design, Development and Preliminary Testing phase and systematically proceed through the project. This process would be repeated until all functionality is completed and delivered.

This iterative approach is one of the most valuable processes I have learned for starting a small project and incorporating additional items as the project grows. Too often, I see projects flounder because no one on the team was able to wrap their arms around the project and take ownership. This scenario results in a project that is in disarray, with frustrated team members and disappointing results for you, the Project Manager, the team and the entire organization.

Along the same lines, I have seen a number of projects fail because of a lack of support from multiple departments. My suggestion again is to start small, even if it is just you, and then as other groups see the benefit, include them in the project. This is especially true with IT projects where you may get little to no support for a project at the early stages. Once a small number of people are using the technology and see the benefits, then they want, and even sometimes demand, the technology to be implemented for their staff. When this occurs, you have a much different problem to solve, but this book will outline some suggestions to manage the expectations.

General Project Management Phases

After managing a number of IT projects, I have adopted a hybrid version of the SDLC and RAD methodologies (outlined in the previous section). Table 2.2 provides additional details for the recommended phases, description, staff and deliverables.

ID	Phases	Description	Team Members	Deliverables
1	Project Scope	• Determine the overall business need, project goals, team members, time frame and budget for the initiative. • Gain Executive level support for the project.	• Stakeholders • Project Manager	• Project Scope Documentation • Project Scope Sign-Off
2	Project Break Down	• Translate the Project Scope into a tangible project plan to provide to the team in the next phase. • Build basic documentation templates for the Project and reuse existing organization information (policies, procedures, standards, etc.) for future phases. • Determine the Communication Plan for the project. • Determine general Roles and Responsibilities for the project.	• Project Manager	• Project Plan – Rev 1 • Project Administration Templates • Pre-Existing Documentation that may be crucial • Communication Plan

Table 2.2: General Project Management Phases.

ID	Phases	Description	Team Members	Deliverables
3	Kick-Off Meeting	• Assemble the entire team to review the Project Scope, Project Plan, Core Documents and Communication Plan. • Build momentum and excitement for the project. • Obtain consensus with commitments for a successful project.	• Stakeholders • Entire IT Team • Project Manager • Users	• Project Plan – Rev 2 • Project Team is in-sync
4	Requirements Analysis	• Determine core functionality and modules to complete the application. • Finalize project time line, deliverables and project team.	• Stakeholders • Entire IT Staff • Project Manager	• Requirements Analysis Documentation • Communication Plan • Roles and Responsibilities • Cost – Benefit Analysis • Feasibility Analysis • Requirements Analysis Sign-Off
5	Design, Development and Preliminary Testing	• Translate the Requirements Analysis into a functional design. • Develop the Application or Process from the Functional Design. • Application or Process Review • Set up necessary hardware and software environments for testing purposes. • Perform baseline testing to verify the Application or Process meets the Requirements Analysis.	• Developers • DBAs • Users	• Technology Design • Operational Processes • Application Code • Preliminary Testing Plan • Preliminary Testing Exception • Design and Development Sign-Off
6	Formal Testing	• Perform Functional Testing to satisfy the Requirements. • Perform Integration Testing among existing infrastructure and business components. • Perform Load Testing of the system to ensure acceptable performance at peak times. • Perform User Acceptance Testing to verify the system can be used efficiently and accurately by the User Community.	• Testers • Developers • DBAs • Users	• Formal Testing Plan • Formal Testing Exceptions • Testing Sign-Off

Table 2.2: General Project Management Phases (continued).

ID	Phases	Description	Team Members	Deliverables
7	Finalize Documentation	• Polish documentation in order to capture historical information.	• Entire Team	• Comprehensive System Documentation
8	User Training	• Build training material and teach the User Community the system features.	• Trainers • Users	• Trained Users • Training Sign-Off
9	GO | NO GO Meeting	• Ensure the entire team is confident the implementation will be successful and no issues will hamper the implementation.	• Entire Team	• Pre Impletation Sign-off
10	Implementation	• Implement system. • Validate system implementation via Functional Testing.	• Entire Team	• Implemented System • Post Implementation Sign-Off
11	Lessons Learned Meeting	• Determine project successes and failures that can be improved upon for future projects.	• Entire Team	• Lessons Learned • Project Completion Survey
12	Maintenance	• Execute processes on a regular interval to ensure the system will perform properly.	• IT Staff	• Properly maintained system

Table 2.2: General Project Management Phases (continued).

If your organization has already committed to either the SDLC or RAD methodology, the techniques in this book can be followed with either approach. Both methodologies follow the same functional steps, but the RAD methodology incorporates more of an iterative approach during the Design, Development and Testing phases, while the SDLC Methodology completes each of these steps individually before proceeding to the next step.

Practically speaking, the technical staff meets with Users at particular points in the project to make sure that the needs are being addressed. With these interactions, the process naturally lends itself to the RAD or Hybrid methodology I have suggested. Some projects are planned to have the core functionality designed, developed, tested and implemented. Once this is completed, the design, development and testing are conducted for the next set of bells and whistles.

The scale and duration comprising the level of effort for the project may dictate the depth of the project phases and the details associated with project documentation. Although the process remains the same, for a week-long project involving two people, a skeletal set of documents may suffice with less emphasis on formal communication. A project with more team members, a longer duration, and more risk would require a full set of detailed documents to facilitate collaboration and project implementation.

Project Example – SQL Server 2000 Upgrade Project Phases

From the comprehensive project phases, we move to the high level SQL Server 2000 Upgrade Project Phases needed to complete the project. Based on the SQL Server Upgrade project example, Table 2.3. outlines my recommended phases for completing the project accurately. The phases in this table occur in the sequence listed. For each phase, the table shows the corresponding documentation which will be discussed throughout the remainder of this book, and also the project documents that should be leveraged throughout the course of the project.

SQL Server 6.5 to 2000 Upgrade Phases	

PROJECT DOCUMENTS LEVERAGED THROUGHOUT THE PROJECT:

- **Project Plan**

- **Issues List**

- **Communication Plan**

- **Agenda Minutes**

- **Roles and Responsibilities**

PROJECT WORKFLOW FOR SQL SERVER 6.5 TO 2000 UPGRADE

ID	Phase	Documentation
1	Project Scope	Project Scope, Cost Benefit
2	Project Break Down	Project Plan
3	Kick Off Meeting	
4	Requirements Analysis	Requirements Analysis
5	Upgrade Design	Upgrade Plan
6	Pre-Upgrade Testing	
7	Environment Setup	Server Spec
8	User, Function, Load Testing	Testing Plans, Testing Exceptions
9	Code Modifications	Program Updates
10	GO/NO GO Meeting	
11	SQL Server Upgrade	Checklist
12	Lessons Learned Meeting	Project Survey

Table 2.3: General Project Management Phases for SQL Server 2000 Upgrade Example.

Lessons Learned

▶ In order to achieve success, Project Managers require interpersonal, technical, managerial and communication skills.

▶ The Project Management Life Cycle is a comprehensive process that most likely exists in your organization, but needs to be formalized and refined.

▶ In each phase, it is necessary to determine the goals, deliverables, documentation and team members based on your project needs, if the project is to scale appropriately.

Chapter 3

Project Scope

"On the clarity of your ideas depends the scope of your success in any endeavor."
—James Robertson

Organizations have many initiatives that may 1) improve operational efficiencies; 2) reduce costs; 3) generate revenue; 4) deliver a public service; and 5) prove compliance with industry standards. Each item is a core need for every business throughout all industries. With businesses relying on technology to address these initiatives, IT Departments fall in line to these business needs and often become the catalyst for successfully migrating these initiatives into organizational projects. The IT Project Manager often learns of the Business Vision from Senior IT Management and begins to scope the needed project.

The first phase of managing an IT project is to refine the Project Vision into a viable Project Scope that is easily understood. Most often, the Project Scope is started informally and then refined into a formal set of project goals. By formalizing this stage of the project, it is simple to define the project boundaries, and steer the remainder of the project to a reasonable set of expectations. Setting goals and expectations early in the project is imperative to ensure that goals are achieved that will benefit the business and resolve the issue at hand.

At this early stage in the project, it is necessary to earn the support of top level executives who will back and fund the overall project. It is imperative that these individuals understand the business benefits derived from completing the project. Once their support is earned, it must be retained and often strengthened for the duration of the project. Unless top level management understands the project's quantitative and qualitative benefits, they may question its overall merit and fail to support it at critical points.

The Project Vision statement must be a simple statement that the entire group can rally behind. As the project begins, this short statement should become the 'Team Rally Statement' for the project. This statement should elicit excitement from the entire team as an opportunity to successfully implement a solution that will benefit the organization. This statement should be revisited during the course of the project to ensure it is progressing on the right path in an efficient manner.

Each team member should be able to wrap their arms around a set of tangible and feasible project goals that derive from the Project Vision. To resolve the business need, these project goals should consist of Functionality, Cost and Time Frame. A Cost Benefit Analysis can often help to quantify the aspects of the project that are vital to its efficiency. A Feasibility Analysis can also convince the Stakeholders that the tools to build the solution are available and can support the Cost Benefit Analysis.

The final aspect of the Project Scope is to define the project team at least at a departmental level, if not at an individual level. For example, the SQL Server 2000 Upgrade team should consist of the Stakeholders, Users, Testers, Network Administrators, Desktop Technicians, Developers, DBAs and any additional staff needed to successfully complete the project.

Planning and preparing for IT Projects should not be understated or undervalued by organizations. According to some accounts, for every dollar or hour spent in the project planning stages, five dollars or hours is saved across the life of the project. To realize the time and cost savings that come from proper planning, it is necessary to have a clear understanding of the business needs. Once the needs are clearly understood, the staff must focus on a quality solution to efficiently and accurately resolve those needs.

Let me give you one example of poor planning and careless spending. In an infrastructure project I am aware of, the team was instructed by the Stakeholders to "just get the work done." The team understood and shared this perspective. They worked very quickly and cut many corners to get the job done as directed by the Stakeholders. This project resulted in a long-term, nagging maintenance problem and a huge thorn in the department's side.

At the organization, the project was known to require extensive reworking and maintenance. The ongoing system maintenance cost more time and money than if the project had been addressed properly in the first place. To add insult to injury, the team dreaded working on this infrastructure component and the company lost confidence in the IT department. This caused greater stress between the business units and hindered the working relationship. If you are going to address a business need with an IT Project, I recommend taking pride in completing it properly the first time. This will save the company time and money, and give you the opportunity to address new projects.

As shown in Table 3.1, the Project Vision is a single statement that anyone in the organization can understand. This concise statement identifies the key aspects of the project: Who, What, Where, When, Why and How. Table 3.1 shows the project goals, which are also tangible and understandable by all members of the project team. Hyperlinks are used as references to the existing Cost Benefit and Feasibility Analysis documents, and serve as additional information for the project team.

Figure 3.1 shows the applicable Project Plan tasks for the Project Scope Phase. Details of breaking down a project are outlined in Chapter 4.

	ⓘ	Task Name	Duration	Start	Finish	Prede	% Complet	Resource Names
1		⊟ SQL Server 6.5 to 2000 Upgrade	40 days	Mon 11/4/02	Fri 12/27/02		0%	
2		⊟ Project Scope	4 days	Mon 11/4/02	Thu 11/7/02		0%	
3	▦	Project Scope Meeting	1 day	Mon 11/4/02	Mon 11/4/02		0%	Project Manager
4	▨	Determine Key Staff, Stakeholders, Budget and Goals	1 day	Mon 11/4/02	Mon 11/4/02		0%	Project Manager
5	▨	Compile the Feasibility Analysis	1 day	Tue 11/5/02	Tue 11/5/02	4	0%	Project Manager
6	▨	Calculate the Cost Benefit Analysis	1 day	Wed 11/6/02	Wed 11/6/02	5	0%	Project Manager
7		Project Scope Review and Editing	1 day	Thu 11/7/02	Thu 11/7/02	6	0%	Project Manager,Stakeholders
8	▨	Project Scope Sign-Off	0 days	Thu 11/7/02	Thu 11/7/02	7	0%	Stakeholders
9		⊞ Requirements Analysis	7 days	Fri 11/8/02	Mon 11/18/02	2	0%	
17		⊞ Test Environment Setup	5 days	Tue 11/19/02	Mon 11/25/02	9	0%	

Figure 3.1: Project Plan — Project Scope Tasks.

SQL Server 6.5 to 2000 Upgrade Project Scope

Project Vision
- Upgrade the core business system in our office from SQL Server 6.5 to 2000 in less than two months with existing company resources, resulting in equivalent or better overall system performance.

Project Goals
- Meet all deadlines listed in the Project Plan.
- Upgrade to better performance than the SQL Server 6.5 environment.
- Minimize the downtime needed for the upgrade.
- Free-flowing communication will enable the team to work closely.
- Have this project serve as a test bed for future projects with a similar format.

Project Scope
- Upgrade the single system with no further functionality, but improve performance as needed, based on the testing results.

Analysis
- Cost Benefit Analysis—Quantitative and Qualitative Analysis
- Feasibility Analysis—Financial, Staffing, Technical and Legal Analysis

Cost
- Leverage existing staff and testing equipment.
- Purchase a new production server and licenses.

Time Frame
- Two months, starting ASAP.

Stakeholders
- The Company
- Operations Department—Users
- Development Department
- DBA Department

Staff
- Management
- Developers
- Network Administrators
- Testers
- Users
- DBAs

Table 3.1: Phase Document — Project Scope.

Cost Benefit Analysis

A typical scenario that I hear from many IT Professionals is that upper level management does not understand the latest and greatest technology and they are unwilling to approve a project because of the cost. I want to provide suggestions for this scenario to show the benefits in terms that Executives understand. Too often, when technical staff tries to pitch to IT Management or 'C' level Executives, they are rejected because they talk about the new and "cool" features rather than the financial and business benefits that can be derived from the project. This communication problem stems from not recognizing the audience and its interests, and from failing to communicate how the project relates to the overall organization.

Table 3.2 shows a Cost Benefit Analysis for the SQL Server 2000 Upgrade, as an example of how the IT staff can demonstrate the project's merits in terms that Executives can understand. In order to determine the true cost to the company, this Cost Benefit Analysis is comprised of both quantitative and qualitative factors. Quantitative figures can be tangibly measured and have an associated dollar figure. Qualitative figures are intangible and typically do not have a precise measurement. These items are typically assessed according to their impact on the organization. In this scenario, they are measured as High, Medium or Low.

Quantitative Costs	Amount		Quantitative Benefits	Amount
Server Hardware *(4 CPU, 2 GB RAM, 6 Disks, Controllers)*	$30,000.00		User Time Savings Per Year *(Greater Transactions per Users)*	$100,000.00
SQL Server Licensing *(4 Per CPU Standard Edition Licenses)*	$20,000.00		Technical Staff Efficiencies *(Daily Processes and New Capabilities)*	$50,000.00
Project Team Salary and Benefits *(2 Months Project Team Expenses)*	$200,000.00		Prior Downtime Costs *(50 Hours * $10,000 Per Hour)*	$500,000.00
Total	$250,000.00		Total	$650,000.00
			Return on Investment	*$400,000.00*

Qualitative Costs	Amount		Qualitative Benefits	Amount
Opportunity Cost for other Projects	1		Reliability for New Biz Opportunities	3
Perception Systems are Unstable	2		System Performance	3
Frustrated User Base	1		Architecture Scalability	3
Persistent IT Staff Firefighting	1		New SQL Server Features	3
Limited Functionality	1		Expanded Third Party Tools	3
Average	6		Average	15

LEGEND - QUALITATIVE COSTS\BENEFITS		*Return on Investment*	*15/6 = 2.5*
1 = Low			
2 = Medium			
3 = High			

Table 3.2: Phase Document — Cost Benefit Analysis - SQL Server 2000 Upgrade Project.

In the scenario outlined in Table 3.2, the quantitative costs are $250,000, with the benefits amounting to $650,000. This yields a quantitative Return on Investment (ROI) of $400,000. The qualitative analysis is calculated on a three point scale where 1 = Low, 2 = Medium and 3 = High. The qualitative costs equal 6, while the qualitative benefits equal 15. The qualitative ROI is calculated by dividing the benefit by the cost, which in this example equals 2.5. This is a Medium to High qualitative ROI.

Feasibility Analysis

Once the Executive Management begins to support the project, the Project Manager must assess some of the key project components prior to any significant investments of time or money. This assessment should reassure Executive Management and serve as an example of due diligence.

During one project I managed, I formalized the project team among three Directors in the IT Department. The three Directors planned to have staff working on the project in different capacities. Two Directors immediately agreed with the project goals, while the third Director was absolutely opposed. The third Director believed that the goal of the project was not technically feasible, based on a previous project and on the line of technology products to be used.

Due to the major rift among the Directors, I developed a series of questions for the staff. I wanted to make sure we were going in the right direction and that we were all on the same page. At the same time, I conducted some Web research for success stories related to the project goals. Once I compiled the results from the questionnaires and included the success stories, I spoke with the third Director about the technology in relation to the project goals. The information from the team and the Web research convinced the third Director that the project goals were feasible and the risk was low for the organization, because other companies had already paved the way.

Table 3.3 outlines a baseline feasibility analysis for the SQL Server 2000 Upgrade. It is intended to address Financial, Staffing, Technical and Legal considerations for the project. These questions require input from all of the Stakeholders, and ultimately, agreement among the Stakeholders to ensure that time and money are not carelessly allocated to an impossible project.

ID	Cat.	Question	Answer
1	Financial	Do we have a sufficient budget to pay for the project?	
2	Financial	⊠ill the company derive both quantitative and qualitative benefits from the project?	
3	Staffing	Are internal staff members available to address this project and do they have the necessary experience?	
4	Staffing	Are external consultants necessary?	
5	Technical	Is the technology available and performing reliably in the industry?	
6	Technical	Do we have a clear upgrade path from our existing platform to the future platform?	
7	Technical	Has an accurate and efficient process been developed to work through the upgrade process?	
8	Technical	Have other companies been successful with this type of project and how did they complete it?	
9	Technical	Do we need to reach a 'make' or 'buy' decision?	
10	Legal	⊠ill we face any legal implications with the project?	
11	Misc	Additional considerations?	
12	Misc	Outstanding items?	

FINAL DECISION (Start Project, Further Research, Do not Start Project)	
RATIONALE	

Prepared By: _____   Title: _____

Signature: _____   Date: _____

Table 3.3: Phase Document — SQL Server 6.5 to 2000 Upgrade Feasibility Analysis.

Once the Project Scope is compiled, you must provide the information to the Stakeholders and request Sign-Off on the phase in order to continue with the Project Breakdown phases. Once unanimous agreement is reached, it is time for you as the Project Manager to translate this information into a Project Plan and begin working with the technical staff. The Project Manager must start the momentum and work with staff members to meet or exceed the project goals.

Lessons Learned

▶ The Project Scope is intended to serve as a boundary for the project that is easily understood and accepted by all team members as a general vision whose overall goal is to benefit the organization.

▶ Planning cannot be underestimated. According to some accounts, for every dollar spent during the planning stages of the project, five dollars is saved across the life of the project.

▶ The Cost Benefit Analysis can be calculated both quantitatively and qualitatively in order to determine the benefits derived from the project in real dollars.

▶ The Feasibility Analysis is a measure of due diligence by the project team to verify that the company can benefit from the project from a business, technical, legal and regulatory perspective.

FREE *Bonus:*

Sample Project Scope and Feasibility documents are available as free downloads when you register your book at www.rationalpress.com.

Chapter 4

Project Plan Break Down

"Good plans shape good decisions. That's why good planning helps to make elusive dreams come true." —Lester R. Bittel

Typically, one of the most difficult components for Project Managers from a procedural perspective is related to building the project plan. During the Project Breakdown stage, the Project Manager's primary goal is to build a Project Plan at a granular level, with each task assigned to an individual on the team. Unfortunately, both new and experienced Project Managers have a difficult time completing this goal because a standardized process has not yet been defined to tangibly build it. This chapter is intended to alleviate the problem of "getting the plan down on paper."

Follow these steps to efficiently and accurately build project plans:

- ▶ Determine Major Project Phases

- ▶ Expand Tasks to Finer Granularity

- ▶ Determine Task Time Frame and Responsibility

- ▶ Finalize First Revision Project Plan

- ▶ Obtain a Reality Check

The following sections elaborate on each of these steps to break down a project. The descriptions are intended to serve as repeatable processes for future projects. In each of these sections, a brief description will be provided with examples from the SQL Server 2000 Upgrade.

Determine Major Project Phases

In some respects, all good projects start with a clean slate. When starting a project, it is not necessary to use an expensive project management tool. A white board or a blank sheet of paper will suffice. Use this time to brainstorm about the major milestones associated with this project and jot down your ideas on paper, as shown in Table 4.1.

IDEAS FOR THE SQL SERVER 2000 UPGRADE – 11.01.2002
1. Scope and the general requirements
2. Find servers for testing and production
3. See who I can work with on the project
4. Testing for the Upgrade
5. Talk to Management for support and ideas
6. Figure out the schedule and budget
7. Compile the project docs
8. Put together the upgrade plan
9. Talk about user training

Table 4.1: Project Plan — Brainstorming and Idea Generation.

Once your general ideas are in writing, it is time to migrate them to a high level plan. The project plan in Figure 4.1 is an early version of the SQL Server 2000 Upgrade project plan.

	❶	Task Name	Duration	Start	Finish
1		Project Scope	1 day	Mon 11/4/02	Mon 11/4/02
2		Determine Key Staff, Stakeholders, Budget and Goals	1 day	Mon 11/4/02	Mon 11/4/02
3		Requirements Analysis	1 day	Tue 11/5/02	Tue 11/5/02
4		Kick Off Meeting	1 day	Mon 11/4/02	Mon 11/4/02
5		Identify, Order and Obtain Hardware Needed	1 day	Mon 11/4/02	Mon 11/4/02
6		Develop Test Plans	1 day	Mon 11/4/02	Mon 11/4/02
7		Determine Communication Procedure	1 day	Mon 11/4/02	Mon 11/4/02
8		Setup Hardware	1 day	Mon 11/4/02	Mon 11/4/02
9		Functional, Load, End UserTesting	1 day	Mon 11/4/02	Mon 11/4/02
10		SQL Server Upgrade	1 day	Mon 11/4/02	Mon 11/4/02
11		Lessons Learned	1 day	Mon 11/4/02	Mon 11/4/02

Figure 4.1: Project Plan — Major Milestone Tasks in Microsoft Project.

These major milestone tasks should be sufficient to start the project based on an early understanding of the project requirements. Once high level tasks are identified, it is time to start thinking about gaps between the tasks. Think about how you would complete the project one step at a time and record these thoughts. Do not be concerned if these tasks are not 100% coherent; at this stage in the process, rely on brainstorming to determine the tasks.

Expand Tasks to Finer Granularity

Once the major milestones are identified, it may be beneficial to move to a Project Management Tool, such as Microsoft Project. At this stage, begin to create Phase Summary Tasks and Sub Tasks based on the project phases. The ultimate goal is to have each task organized from start to finish, with each task assigned to a single individual. Try to define as many tasks as possible, with the realization that other team members will add more tasks later for a comprehensive project plan.

In Figure 4.2, the Phase Summary Tasks are shown in bold type, as represented by Tasks 1 and 4. Sub Tasks are indented and in plain type. The Project Manager should assign Sub Tasks to individuals, but not the Phase Summary Tasks. The Phase Summary Tasks will serve as Duration aggregates as well as phase start and finish dates as the project plan is fine-tuned in the next few steps.

The Project Plan snippet in Figure 4.2 shows the early stages of the Project Scope and Requirements Analysis and the associated tasks.

	❶	Task Name	Duration	Start	Finish
1		⊟ **Project Scope**	**1 day**	**Mon 11/4/02**	**Mon 11/4/02**
2		Project Scope Meeting	1 day	Mon 11/4/02	Mon 11/4/02
3		Determine Key Staff, Stakeholders, Budget and Goals	1 day	Mon 11/4/02	Mon 11/4/02
4		⊟ **Requirements Analysis**	**1 day**	**Tue 11/5/02**	**Tue 11/5/02**
5		Kick Off Meeting	1 day	Tue 11/5/02	Tue 11/5/02
6		Identify, Order and Obtain Hardware Needed	1 day	Tue 11/5/02	Tue 11/5/02
7		Develop Test Plans	1 day	Tue 11/5/02	Tue 11/5/02
8		Determine SQL Server Configurations and Security	1 day	Tue 11/5/02	Tue 11/5/02
9		Determine Communication Procedure	1 day	Tue 11/5/02	Tue 11/5/02
10		Complete Requirements Analysis Document	1 day	Tue 11/5/02	Tue 11/5/02

Figure 4.2: Project Plan — Project Task Expansion in Microsoft Project.

At this stage in the Project Plan, it is necessary to begin assigning these tasks to single individuals and determine an accurate time frame for the proper completion of each task. I cannot stress enough that each task on the Project Plan should be assigned to a single individual on the team and allocated a feasible time frame. It is best to have a single individual assigned to each detailed task, even if this means having a greater number of tasks. There is no advantage in having fewer, less-detailed tasks if team members are confused about their precise responsibilities.

I have seen two or three team members assigned to a task where each team member assumed the other person was going to complete it. Needless to say, the deliverables were late and this caused problems among the team members. Worse yet is a scenario where a single task requires the attention of multiple individuals, but only one person is assigned the task. In this scenario, rather than the Project Manager addressing the need, the team member tries to convince other individuals to quickly complete the work. Unfortunately, these scenarios ultimately cause project delays and would be better managed if the Project Manager assigned the tasks to a single individual and managed the progress.

Do not be afraid to have a long project plan if many individuals are required to complete the tasks. It is better to err on the side of over-planning when you are new to Project Management or to the team, than to overlook key items based on an assumption. As you manage more projects and build rapport with the team, a happy medium will naturally flow from you to the project plan and then to the team. The same principles can apply to calculating the Duration on a per task basis, as outlined in the next section.

Determine Task Time Frame and Responsibility

As the Sub Tasks are defined, begin estimating the amount of time necessary to complete those tasks. This estimate is called the Duration, as shown in Figure 4.3. The correct Duration will provide an accurate indication of the level of effort for a particular task, based on the project resources. The Duration will also provide the total time frame needed to complete each task and the overall project.

Based on your experience, assess the Duration required to complete each task. Feel comfortable slightly overestimating the Duration if you are not familiar with the time needed. A reasonable overestimation factor of 20% can be incorporated for some tasks if you are uncertain. To accurately assess the Duration, ask team members about their level of confidence to complete the tasks within the allocated Duration.

	❶	Task Name	Duration	Start	Finish	Predecessors	% Complete	Resource Names
1		⊟ **Project Scope**	**3 days**	**Mon 11/4/02**	**Wed 11/6/02**		0%	
2		Project Scope Meeting	1 day	Mon 11/4/02	Mon 11/4/02		0%	Project Manager
3		Determine Key Staff, Stakeholders, Budget and Goals	3 days	Mon 11/4/02	Wed 11/6/02		0%	Project Manager
4		⊟ **Requirements Analysis**	**7 days**	**Thu 11/7/02**	**Fri 11/15/02**	**1**	0%	
5		Kick Off Meeting	1 day	Thu 11/7/02	Thu 11/7/02		0%	Project Manager
6		Identify, Order and Obtain Hardware Needed	7 days	Thu 11/7/02	Fri 11/15/02		0%	Network Admin
7		Develop Test Plans	7 days	Thu 11/7/02	Fri 11/15/02		0%	Tester
8		SQL Server Configurations and Security	7 days	Thu 11/7/02	Fri 11/15/02		0%	DBA
9		Determine Communication Procedure	1 day	Thu 11/7/02	Thu 11/7/02		0%	Project Manager
10		Complete Requirements Analysis Document	7 days	Thu 11/7/02	Fri 11/15/02		0%	Project Manager

Figure 4.3: Project Plan — Project Tasks with Time Frame and Responsibility in Microsoft Project.

In conjunction with Duration, it is necessary to determine the Predecessors for the phases of the project. The **Predecessor** column in Figure 4.3 indicates the order in which tasks must be completed for the project. As a new Project Manager, it is a good idea to set up the Predecessor relationships between Project Summary Tasks to ensure that sequential tasks are properly completed.

With the combination of the Duration and the Predecessors, it is necessary to establish deadlines for each task and the overall project. It is the first goal of the Project Scope to meet all the deadlines set forth in the Project Plan. Make sure the Durations are feasible by verifying them with the team. Your team should be able to confirm their commitment to the prescribed dates based on the project requirements, additional organizational projects and personal schedules. With an agreement among the team members, use the deadlines as a motivating factor for the Team and as a credibility indicator.

The **% Complete** column in Figure 4.3 should be updated as the project progresses. These percentages should be updated by the individual team member assigned to the Sub Task. The assigned team member is listed in the **Resource Names** column in Figure 4.3.

During these early stages of the project, it is advantageous for the Project Manager to list a generic team member if individual team members have not yet been identified. By doing this, it is at least possible to determine the amount of time needed to perform the task. This information can help Personnel Managers and Executive Management to understand the level of effort on the part of team members over the course of the project.

Finalize First Revision Project Plan

From the earlier steps in the Project Breakdown, the following items should have been accomplished:

▶ All major project phases have been identified as Phase Summary Tasks.

▶ Known Sub Tasks have been identified for each Phase Summary Task.

▶ Sub Tasks are granular enough to assign a single individual to the task.

▶ The Duration is determined for each Sub Task.

▶ Predecessors are established between each Phase Summary Task.

▶ Generic Team Members are identified for each Sub Task if the team member has not been identified.

To finalize the First Revision of the Project Plan, it is necessary to incorporate the following additional items (each bullet corresponds to Figure 4.4):

▶ Insert a Project Summary Task on the first line of the Project Plan that summarizes the Duration, Project Start and Finish Dates for the entire project.

▶ Incorporate meeting times in the Project Plan. Choose a consistent day and time and reserve the appointments on each team member's calendar. Reserve a meeting room to avoid any conflicts.

▶ Leverage Hyperlinks (which appear in Figure 4.4 as globes with chain links) in the Project Plan as references to existing documentation available in the organization or on the Internet.

▶ Incorporate Phase Sign-Off as the milestone for each phase. An example of this is shown as Task 13 of Figure 4.4.

	○	Task Name	Duration	Start	Finish	Predecessors	% Complete	Resource Names
1		⊟ SQL Server 6.5 to 2000 Upgrade	38 days	Mon 11/4/02	Wed 12/25/02		0%	
2		⊞ Project Scope	3 days	Mon 11/4/02	Wed 11/6/02		0%	
6		⊟ Requirements Analysis	7 days	Thu 11/7/02	Fri 11/15/02	2	0%	
7		Kick Off Meeting	1 day	Thu 11/7/02	Thu 11/7/02		0%	Project Manager
8		Identify, Order and Obtain Hardware	7 days	Thu 11/7/02	Fri 11/15/02		0%	Network Admin
9	⊕	Develop Test Plans	7 days	Thu 11/7/02	Fri 11/15/02		0%	Tester
10	⊕	SQL Server Configurations and Security	7 days	Thu 11/7/02	Fri 11/15/02		0%	DBA
11	⊕	Determine Communication Procedure	1 day	Thu 11/7/02	Thu 11/7/02		0%	Project Manager
12	⊕	Complete Requirements Analysis	7 days	Thu 11/7/02	Fri 11/15/02		0%	Project Manager
13	⊕	Requirements Analysis Sign-Off	0 days	Fri 11/15/02	Fri 11/15/02	12	0%	Stakeholders
14		⊞ Test Environment Setup	5 days	Mon 11/18/02	Fri 11/22/02	6	0%	
18		⊞ Preliminary Upgrade Testing	3 days	Mon 11/25/02	Wed 11/27/02	17	0%	
23		⊞ Production Environment Setup	5 days	Mon 11/25/02	Fri 11/29/02	14	0%	
27		⊞ Functional Testing	6 days	Mon 12/2/02	Mon 12/9/02	26	0%	
32		⊞ Load Testing	5 days	Thu 12/5/02	Wed 12/11/02	29	0%	
37		⊞ End User Testing	5 days	Wed 12/11/02	Tue 12/17/02	34	0%	
42		⊟ SQL Server Upgrade	3 days	Wed 12/18/02	Fri 12/20/02	41	0%	
43		Go	No Go Meeting	1 day	Wed 12/18/02	Wed 12/18/02		0%	Project Manager
44	📅	⊞ SQL Server 6.5 to 2000 Upgrade	1 day	Fri 12/20/02	Fri 12/20/02		0%	
50		⊞ Lessons Learned	3 days	Mon 12/23/02	Wed 12/25/02	42	0%	

Figure 4.4: Project Plan — First Revision Project Plan in Microsoft Project.

▶ Identify milestones. These are significant events in the project and have a Duration of 0 Days on the Project Plan. They identify when the project can move to the next phase. An example of a milestone is Task 13 in Figure 4.4.

▶ Establish Date Constraints for the Sub Tasks to realistically set time frame expectations, such as "Must Start On" or "Must End On." These are represented by a Calendar symbol, as seen in Task 44 in Figure 4.4.

▶ Associate a Sub Task document that must be prepared, or a Hyperlink to existing documentation. A Note can be associated with the task to store simple text information. This Note is represented by a yellow Post-It Note symbol, as seen in Task 44 in Figure 4.4.

Obtain a Reality Check

Once you as the Project Manager have completed the First Revision of the Project Plan, it is sensible to seek advice from others in your organization to validate the information. Spending 30 to 60 minutes with another person to evaluate the plan will mitigate risk and encourage overall project endorsement. Be sure to evaluate the following items:

▶ Confirm realistic Durations for tasks and for the entire project.

▶ Uncover overlooked tasks to round-off the project.

▶ Identify proper Predecessors among the various tasks.

▶ Validate accurate task assignments to Team Members.

For this information, I recommend speaking with one or two people rather than the entire group. Save the group feedback for the Kick-Off Meeting. Depending on the project and organization policies, it may be a good idea to discuss the plan with a subject matter expert (either internal or external to your organization) with whom you have a personal-professional relationship. The extra set of eyes can reap numerous benefits.

Lessons Learned

▶ An iterative approach is necessary to build project plans. Start small and then build a comprehensive Project Plan to address organizational needs.

▶ To avoid confusion and ensure that tasks are completed on time, make certain that each task on the Project Plan is assigned to a single individual.

▶ Use Project Management tools to properly establish time frames, dependencies, completion rates and resources.

Chapter 5

Communication Plan

"Communication is something so simple and difficult that we can never put it in simple words."
—T.S. Matthew

We can all figure out the technical aspects when it comes to projects, right? Typically, the major challenge is working with others. This chapter discusses both conventional and unconventional tactics for dealing with this issue. First and foremost, my recommendation for communication is to "build bridges, don't dig ditches."

As the Project Manager, you may have developed the best plan to resolve the business need, but if you cannot communicate the plan and work as a team to achieve the goals, then it will be difficult to achieve success. Communication is a focal point for successful Project Management and must be included in the Project Plan.

You must build a Communication Plan before the project begins. Inform the team of the Communication Plan at the start of the project and include the Communication Plan as a component in the Requirements Analysis Sign-Off.

The following items comprise the major components of the Communication Plan. By following these steps, the team will understand the expectations each member.

▶ Purpose and Expectations

▶ Roles and Responsibilities

► Issues List

► Status Meetings

► Meetings Tips

► Meeting Information

► Project Phase Sign-Offs

► Centralized Project Information

► Keeping the Project on Track

Purpose and Expectations

Now that the expectations for the group have been set in the Project Scope and the project documentation has been reviewed, you must lead by example in all aspects of the project, especially when it comes to communication. Building relationships with the team members is the key to working as an efficient group. Encourage communication among the group whether it is positive, negative or indifferent, but do not praise any communication that is detrimental to the team and its members. In addition, communicate among the project team as well as up, down and across the organization to make sure the necessary individuals are well informed of the project status.

These procedures become essential if and when it is time to communicate any unexpected problems the group may encounter. To prepare for these types of problems, determine who needs to be informed, and at what stage of the problem they should be told. In general, it is best to set expectations early and notify the Stakeholders in anticipation of a problem rather than surprise them with bad news. Few people like surprises, especially if it's bad news.

As the Project Manager, it is imperative that you listen carefully and not jump to conclusions. Communication is 50% speaking and 50% listening, so be sure to address both correctly, especially during critical project phases. When you receive a message, be sure to verify that the message is accurate in order to address it properly.

Another key aspect of communication is how people receive *your* message. Keep in mind that people typically retain information accurately in one of three ways: 1) visual (seeing), 2) verbal (hearing) or 3) kinesthetic (doing). This is very important, because according to some accounts, individuals miss the message they are receiving up to 75% of the time. You must make sure the team communicates properly.

Be sure you are communicating in a manner that best accommodates your team members' preferences, especially on very important matters. If you are working with a new team member and do not know how they prefer their messages, ask the person to identify their preference. If they say "tell me," they are typically verbal; if they say "send me an email," they are typically visual; and if they ask you to "show them," they are typically kinesthetic. Although everyone has all three traits, a person typically has a preference for one particular learning style. Be aware of it and make sure that the team member is receiving information by the means they prefer, especially at critical points in the project.

Be aware of the delivery of your messages. A study at the University of California, Los Angeles a few years ago concluded that the ability of individuals to retain messages is 7% based on the words used, 38% based on voice quality, and 55% based on nonverbal communication. This is an important fact to remember as you deliver key information to your team.

Schedule weekly project meetings at a consistent day of the week and time of day in the same conference room for the entire project. Doing so lessens the confusion about when and where the group is to meet. They will know that the status meeting is always on Tuesdays at 10:00 A.M. ET in the Potomac Room. This also identifies their weekly deadlines for the project. For teams that are geographically dispersed, set up a consistent conference call number for the entire length of the project. Keep the same principles in mind for teams at a single location.

Finally, depending on the length and criticality of the project, take the time to meet the team members face-to-face at their offices to become familiar with them. Consider the trip to be a relationship-building event for this project and for future projects. During this trip, begin to build a strong relationship with the individuals and work to understand the group dynamics. Your goal is to build a relationship and rely on it as the project progresses. There is a higher probability that your team members will want to take the time to work on this particular project if they know who they are working with and if they are confident that there is an open line of communication. If, for example, the project is business critical and will be completed in nine months with 30 staff members at three different sites, it would be beneficial to take the time to visit all three sites and

start the project on a good note rather than make the visit during a crunch time.

Roles and Responsibilities

"You cannot escape the responsibility of tomorrow by evading it today."
– Abraham Lincoln

One of the most detrimental problems team members face is that they do not understand their role in the project. Once a team member sees the Project Plan, they have a basic understanding of project expectations. Unfortunately, too often communication and project problems arise because team members do not understand their responsibilities. Further, team members assume others will be addressing issues that they are responsible for, and the issues end up not being addressed.

This misperception and miscommunication can be easily corrected on a per team member basis by creating a Roles and Responsibility document. This document outlines all of the Roles for the project and what each team member is responsible for in that particular Role. This document provides personal and project accountability by clearly defining the project Roles. Once a baseline set of information is provided, review the contents with the project team for additions or improvements. Verify with the team the accuracy of the Responsibilities per Role, as well as the team members per Role. Also, make sure that everyone is in agreement with their responsibilities.

Table 5.1 shows a sample Roles and Responsibility document for the SQL Server 2000 Upgrade Project. The top portion of the document outlines the Project Roles, while the bottom portion associates a team member to the Role, along with contact information and availability. Having basic contact information included on this one-page document allows quick reference to team members' phone numbers or email addresses.

SQL Server 6.5 to 2000 Upgrade – Project Roles and Responsibilities

PROJECT ROLES

- **Stakeholder** – Develop the Project Scope with the Project Manager and complete Sign-Off at the end of each project phase. Represent each major group involved in the project, including Users, Developers, Network Administration, Testers and DBAs.

- **Project Manager** – ⊠ork toward successful project completion with the available staff and budget. Complete core project documents and verify results from the remainder of the team. Publish the project documents on the project web site.

- **Users** – Execute End User Testing and notify the Project Manager with the results via the End User Exception Document.

- **Network Admin** – Build the Test and Production Servers.

- **Tester** – Execute Functional Testing and notify the Project Manager with the results via the Functional Testing Exception Document. Following the Production SQL Server Upgrade, test the applications with the Functional Test Plan.

- **DBA** – Execute the Preliminary Upgrade Testing Plan, Load Testing Plan and Production SQL Server Upgrade. Notify the Project Manager via the Preliminary Upgrade Exception Document and Load Testing Exception Document, and contribute to certifying the Production SQL Server Upgrade.

PROJECT RESPONSIBILITIES

ID	NAME	ROLE	CONTACT INFO	AVAILABILITY
1	Barbara	Stakeholder – User	x1111	5%
2	Sally	Stakeholder – Developer	x1120	5%
3	John	Stakeholder – Network Admin	x1130	5%
4	Gloria	Stakeholder – Tester	x1140	5%
5	Mike	Stakeholder – DBA	x1150	5%
6	Ted	Project Manager	x1199	75%
7	Heather	User	x1119	10%
8	Joe	Network Admin	x1131	25%
9	Laurie	Tester	x1141	15%
10	Jim	Developer	x1121	25%
11	Dave	DBA	x1151	25%

Table 5.1: Core Project Document — Project Roles and Responsibilities.

One thing to keep in mind is that the Roles and Responsibility document should compliment the Project Plan. That is, the Roles and Responsibility document should outline what a team member should do and the Project Plan should indicate when the low level tasks should be completed. Based on project need, Project Roles can be expanded in the document to incorporate the appropriate level of detail. This can be further supplemented with phase and task level documents which will also have greater detail.

The Roles and Responsibilities document should be reviewed during the Requirements Analysis Status Meeting. To maintain agreement among the team members, the Roles and Responsibilities document should be included in the Requirements Analysis Sign-Off.

Issues List

As the project progresses, issues will arise that need to be addressed to complete the project. An issue is a project risk, potential or actual delays in the project, or problems outside the direct control of the project team that arise during any task or phase of the project. Examples include: budgetary setbacks, hardware availability, programming problems, testing flaws, team member availability, etc. The Issues List is designed to identify, store and track issues.

Based on the criticality of these items, it is imperative for the Project Manager to track the issues and ensure they are all addressed and corrected. With long projects or simultaneous projects, it is easy to overlook and forget problems. The Issues List allows you to have each issue listed with its status identified, which should be reviewed in all status meetings in order to update the team on their progress since the last meeting.

It is prudent to take some time and think of possible issues at the early stages of the project. Have a brainstorming session with your team to think about items that could cause problems for the project. I recommend being reasonable about these items as you think through the project steps with your team members. As items are determined, ask for possible resolutions. This strategy can reap numerous benefits for project success and give some insight into team member concerns. I recommend saving this information for future use and referring back to it often to ensure that the project will not fall victim to any of these problems. However, it may not be advantageous to distribute this information among the team members, because it could cause paranoia or elicit pessimistic dispositions.

When using the Issues List, number each issue and record the information chronologically for a historical record. Identify each entry as 'Open,' 'In Progress,' or 'Closed' to clearly annotate its status, as outlined in Table 5.2. Based on status meetings and updates from team members, the Project Manager must identify issues and assign them to a single team member to resolve based on the date. As time progresses, it will be easy to track the progress to determine if the problem has been properly solved.

SQL SERVER 6.5 TO 2000 UPGRADE – ISSUES						
ID	**DATE**	**ISSUE**	**SEVERITY**	**PROBABILITY**	**STATUS**	**TEAM**
1	11.04.2002	Production Hardware is not available	High	Medium	Open	Joe
	11.11.2002	Ordered Hardware	Medium	Medium	☒IP	Joe
	11.18.2002	Hardware Delivered & Configured	Low	Low	Closed	Joe
2	11.04.2002	The source code cannot be located in VSS	High	High	Open	Jim
	11.11.2002	The source code was retrieved from a tape backup	Low	Low	Closed	Jim
3	11.11.2002	Project Scope signoff not received	High	Low	Open	Ted
	11.18.2002	Project Scope signoff received	High	Low	Closed	Ted
4	11.04.2002	The budget will need to be pooled from Groups	High	Low	Open	Mike
	11.11.2002	Budget pending	High	Medium	☒IP	Mike
	11.18.2002	Budget resolved	Low	Low	Closed	Mike
5	11.18.2002	More DBAs needed	High	Low	Open	Mike

LEGEND:

- ID – Unique identifier
- Date – Date of information
- Issue – Original issue. Updated issue or Final Resolution
- Severity – (High, Medium, Low) Project impact
- Probability – (High, Medium, Low) Probability the issue will impact the Project
- Status – (Open, ☒IP – ☒ork in Progress, Closed)
- Team – Individual on the team who is responsible

Table 5.2: Core Project Document — Issues List.

Ensure that each issue is only assigned to one person, as outlined in the **Team** column in Table 5.2. This person will be responsible for resolving that problem, and can enlist others to help with solving it. Remind them that they are ultimately responsible.

If the project is experiencing a number of issues, it is important to look at the big picture. Consider migrating complex or interrelated issues to the Project Plan as a new phase or as additional tasks of an existing phase. By doing so, you as the Project Manager are now responsible for ensuring that these tasks are resolved in a way that meets the project deadline.

As the issues are determined, record the perceived Severity (or the negative impact) and the Probability (or the likelihood the issue will occur) for each entry. Be sure that the Severity and Probability match the team's assessment. As updates are provided, be sure to verify that both factors remain in check. You as the Project Manager should pay close attention to issues with both a high Severity and Probability that are not being closed promptly to prevent these issues from delaying the project. These issues can quickly cause a ripple effect if they are not closed in an expedited manner.

As the project progresses, do not become overwhelmed with numerous issues. Although problems may not have the most desirable solution, few problems are irresolvable. As the Project Manager, analyze the problem with the team and determine three to five options that might resolve the issue. Review the options and select the best one. If possible, conduct some minor testing to validate the anticipated results. If problems persist, work toward contacting experts that can provide immediate assistance to benefit the project. Use your best judgment as to when the issues should be escalated to maintain the project's momentum.

Set communication expectations among the project team for the items on the Issues List. Encourage team members to immediately notify the Project Manager and applicable team members when an issue is resolved, in order for the corresponding tasks to be completed. Finally, seek commitments during project meetings that the issues will be resolved in a timely manner.

Status Meetings

Depending on the size of the project, Status Meetings should be held at least once per phase or on a weekly basis. These meetings should be included on the Project Plan as a 'check point' for the team. The objective for these meetings is to ensure that the project is on schedule, moving forward and steps are being taken to address the upcoming phases. Although the details of the agenda will change regularly, it is necessary at a high level to review the Meeting Information (Agenda and Minutes), Project Plan, Issues List and Phase Deliverables. This 'check point' for the team should:

▶ Ensure Issues are being closed.

▶ Verify that Project Plan Tasks are being met on time and accurately.

▶ Ensure that the team is reviewing the project documentation.

▶ Ensure that hand-offs are occurring on time with accurate information.

The bottom line for these meetings is simple: ensure proper communication among the team and address all issues that impact the project.

Meeting Tips

The most important communication for a group is the series of project meetings. For those individuals new to IT Project Management, it is critical to hold succinct and productive meetings. Too often, meetings are long, boring, full of tangents, and have no focus; nothing is accomplished. This lack of productivity is the result of too many of the wrong people on the call. As the Project Manager, you need to resolve these issues. Nothing is truer than the statement "time is money." You need to maximize the team's time while minimizing the cost to the organization. Most businesses recognize that meetings are notorious for wasting time, and yet they are necessary for a reasonable level of communication. It is imperative for your success as a Project Manager to ensure that your meetings are productive and categorized as such. The following items are ways to help keep your meetings productive:

▶ **Advanced Agenda Distribution** — The first way to achieve these goals is to distribute the Meeting Agenda (with the date, time and location) a day or a few days prior to the meeting and request that the team be prepared. By giving the team an opportunity to prepare for the meeting, they can contribute positively to the conversation.

▶ **Consistency** — The second series of recommendations relates to consistency. This includes a consistent meeting day, time and room, and a consistent means to participate in the meetings, such as a conference call number or project web site for contributing and obtaining information. Also, keep meetings focused and concise. If a team member introduces a new item that might be considered a tangent, bring the team back to the main purpose of the meeting. Acknowledge the importance of the new item and agree to discuss it in a separate meeting, or if time permits, at the end of the current meeting.

▶ **Time Management** — Respect everyone's time by starting and ending the meetings on schedule.

▶ **Update Project Documentation** — The final step is to follow up the meeting by giving each attendee copies of Minutes, the Issues List and Updated Project Plan by the close of business that day or at the start of the next business day. This is necessary to keep the communication flowing among the team.

Meeting Information

It often happens that decisions are made during a meeting, but with nothing in writing, most of the attendees forget the decisions that were actually made. The purpose of the Meeting Agenda and Minutes is simple: record the meeting name, date/time, the items discussed (with the applicable decisions made) and list of all attendees. Although this is a simple concept, critical decisions (recorded as minutes) are too often not captured and are lost. If you as the Project Manager cannot conduct the meeting *and* record the minutes, ask a team member to record the minutes so that you can properly conduct the meeting. By simply capturing this information, one can save a significant amount of time by verifying that the decision was made (and the project can therefore move forward) or that an item must be revisited. The bottom line is that it is not sensible to rely on your memory for critical decisions. Instead, use this document as an indisputable record of events.

In order to have productive meetings and maximize the team's time, set an agenda before all meetings. Be sure to post the agenda on the Project's Centralized Information Store (discussed later in this chapter) for the team to review prior to the meeting. At the start of the meeting, review the agenda and ask if anyone has additional agenda items that must be covered. Make sure to follow the agenda during the meeting, so that the team focuses on the issues at hand and the meeting ends on time.

During the meeting, record detailed minutes to serve as historical information for decision-making, especially on long projects or when multiple projects are being addressed by the same staff. This strategy will reap numerous benefits on long projects where early decisions determine the course of action for later stages of the project. Unfortunately, people cannot remember everything and important details may be lost in the progress of the project; this could have major implications.

One typical problem related to meeting minutes is that decisions are not made and projects tend to flounder. Combine your leadership and analytical skills to make sure that decisions are made in a timely manner and enforce those decisions if they will benefit the project. If additional analysis and testing is needed, this should be done quickly and efficiently to prevent indecision and poor productivity from harming the team. Table 5.3 shows the SQL Server 2000 Upgrade Meeting Agenda and Minutes.

SQL SERVER 6.5 TO 2000 UPGRADE – MEETING AGENDA AND MINUTES						
ID	Name	Date/Time	Location	Agenda	Minutes	
1	Project Scope Meeting	11.04.2002 10:00 AM ET	Potomac Room – Number 888.888.8888 Pass Code 12345	• Determine Project Scope • Determine Key Groups • Determine Budget • Determine Project Goals	• Upgrade the business system from SQL Server 6.5 to 2000 • Completed Roles and Responsibilities • Budget determined during project – Issues List • Review Project Plan & Requirements	Barbara, Sally, John, Gloria, Mike, Ted
2	Kick Off Meeting	11.07.2002 10:00 AM ET	Potomac Room – Number 888.888.8888 Pass Code 12345	• Outline Project Goals • Roles & Responsibilities • Review Project Plan & Issues List ⊠eb Site • Additional Items As Needed	• Reviewed Project Plan, Requirements Analysis, and Roles and Responsibilities • See Issues List • Project URL myco.com/652000Upg/	Barbara, Sally, John, Gloria, Mike, Ted, Heather, Joe, Laurie, Jim, Dave
3	Status Meeting	11.14.2002 10:00 AM ET	Potomac Room – Number 888.888.8888 Pass Code 12345	• Review Project Plan • Review Issues List • Review Requirements Analysis		

Table 5.3: Core Project Document — Meeting Agenda and Meeting Minutes.

Project Phase Sign-Offs

For Stakeholders who are not involved in the project details (and perhaps not all of the meetings), but who are responsible for approving the project, it is necessary to ensure that they Sign-Off on the project deliverables for project accountability. This accountability can be achieved by simple Sign-Off at the completion of each phase. Unfortunately, Sign-Offs are typically not incorporated into project planning and can cause great delays if there are disagreements among the team. Be sure to incorporate Sign-Off at the end of each phase to prevent approval problems.

The impact can be even greater in organizations where numerous projects are conducted in adjacent time frames and have dependencies or inputs and outputs among projects. From the Project Manager's perspective, dated Sign-Offs are proof of acceptance and agreement on a per Stakeholder basis. As the Project Manager, you should retain both the original communications sent to the Stakeholders and the responses from each of them.

Any form of written communication can be used to get a phase Sign-Off. It is imperative that you do not use verbal communication, since it does not give you proof of acceptance or rejection. In my experience, it is best to use email for your Sign-Off. Figure 5.1 shows an example Sign-Off email with **Approve/Reject** voting buttons. The body of the email explains the items that are being signed off, when the Sign-Off is needed and how to sign off.

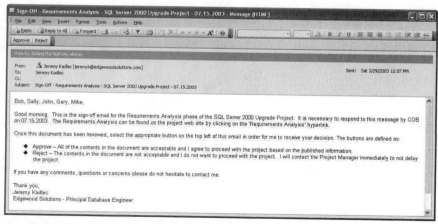

Figure 5.1: Phase Document — Sample Sign-Off Email.

The **Approve/Reject** voting buttons in the email provide an easy way for the Stakeholder to respond to the Sign-Off. All the Stakeholder must do to respond is click on the button of their choosing, which will prompt them to send the message back to you.

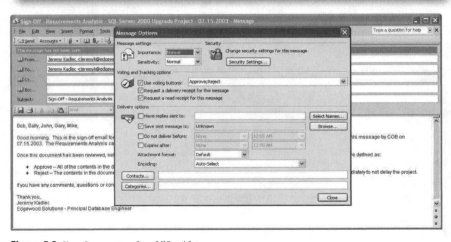

Figure 5.2: Phase Document — Sign-Off Email Setup.

You will receive the Delivery Receipt for the email message when it is processed by the email server. Once the Stakeholder opens the email, you will receive the Read Receipt from the message. Figure 5.3 shows the Read Receipt for the message, outlining that the message was "Read" in the subject line, with the date and time that the message was opened by the recipient.

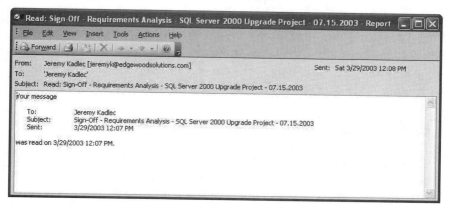

Figure 5.3: Phase Document — Sign-Off Email Read Receipt.

Figure 5.4 shows the response when a Stakeholder selects the **Approve** button from the original email. **Approve:** is added to the subject line of the original email message, as shown in Figure 5.4. As the Project Manager, you should consider this email as your Approval email for the phase.

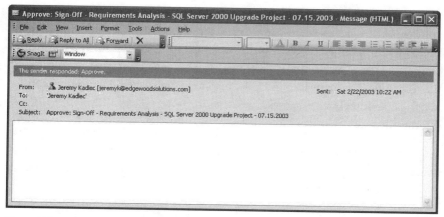

Figure 5.4: Phase Document — Sign-Off Email Approval Response.

As the Project Manager, save all these email messages to and from all Stakeholders to retain the proper Sign-Off documentation for the project. Once all these Sign-Off emails are compiled, they should be stored in the appropriate project folder based on the phase.

One final note: although this functionality is very useful and valuable to the Project Manager, keep in mind that depending on the organization, the email receipts may be blocked by the email server or can even be rejected by the recipient. As such, these messages may not provide a 100% guarantee, so it may be necessary to contact Stakeholders or discuss Sign-Off in phase meetings.

Centralized Project Information

The final component of the Communication Plan is a place to centralize your project information. From a technical perspective, the Centralized Project Information can take on many forms, such as a Windows File System Folder(s), a simple web site, or an Intranet Portal. My recommendation is to start simple and grow. Keep in mind that the goal of the Centralized Project Information is to deliver the content for straightforward communication, rather than implement the technology bells and whistles. If your organization already has a sophisticated web infrastructure for internal projects, take advantage of it; but if this is not available, start small and grow.

Regardless of the technology used and depending on the information that is published, be sure to set up security appropriately. If particular information should not be available to the entire organization, restrict it to internal groups or users. A final best practice is to ensure that each document, regardless of the technology, has a descriptive title, revision number and date/time stamp for historical and tracking purposes.

A reasonable place to start with the Centralized Project Information is with a single file system folder on a corporate share. The root folder can be the project name with child folders for each project phase. The phase documents should be stored in the phase folders, as seen in Figure 5.5.

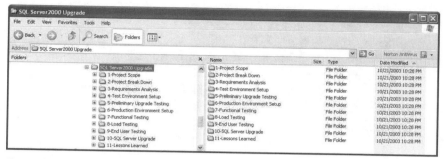

Figure 5.5: Central Project Information — File System Share.

If you can gain access to an internal web server, I recommend a simple web page to centralize your project information. This web site should serve as a common information resource for the project team and entire organization. For the Project Manager, this web site should eliminate version control problems because the entire team can view the same information as long as they review the current web site. Posting the information on the web site will also prevent the email server from flooding with large attachments and confusing the team with frequent updates. It is recommended to send simple email messages to the team indicating when major web site updates have been published, along with the applicable URL. An ideal time to send this email is when you update the web site with the previous status meeting information (Agenda, Minutes, and Issues List). These simple email messages are not only small in size, but can also be discarded by team members once they review the information. All of the major updates to the web site can be saved based on the revision information for historical purposes.

A simple web page can be directly generated from a Word document, which will retain hyperlinks to project documents. As shown in Figure 5.6 and Figure 5.7, highlight the text that should be the Hyperlink, then right-click on the text and choose the **Hyperlink** menu item. The **Insert Hyperlink** dialog box will appear. Type the URL in the **Address** text box on the bottom of the screen and then click the **OK** button to save the Hyperlink.

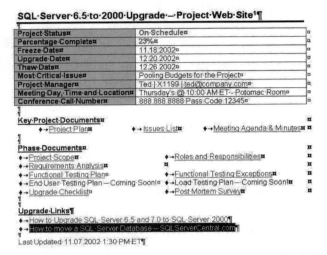

Figure 5.6: Central Project Information — Hyperlink Insertion in Microsoft Word HTML File.

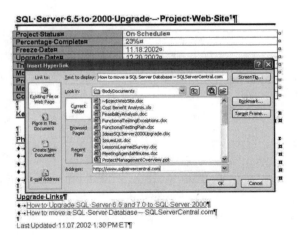

Figure 5.7: Central Project Information — Hyperlink Configuration in Microsoft Word HTML File.

Creating PDF (Portable Document Format) files with Adobe Acrobat is another option for creating HTML files from Microsoft Word. At this point, snapshots of the project documents can be very beneficial for historical purposes. PDF files are a great option for this. A document that reflects the project status at a particular date and time will serve as an effective indicator of project achievements. As the Project Manager generating the PDF files, you will need to use Adobe Acrobat (http://www.adobe.com/products/acrobat/main.html), which is priced as a front office product. Team members do not need to purchase any software, but can download a free version of Acrobat Reader (http://www.adobe.com/products/acrobat/readermain.html) to view the PDF files in a web browser.

In order to create PDF files, it is necessary to install Adobe Acrobat. Once installed, select **Print** from the **File** menu to create the PDF file. In the printer dialog box, left-click on the **Name** drop down box and choose **Acrobat PDFWriter**. Click the **OK** button as shown in Figure 5.8. The **Save PDF File As** dialog box will appear. Select the location to physically save the file in the **Save in** drop down box, as well as name of the file in the **File name** text box, as shown in Figure 5.9.

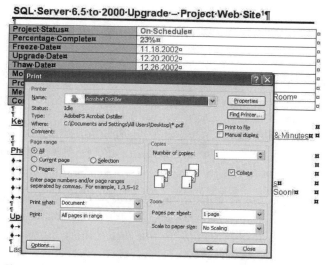

Figure 5.8: Central Project Information — PDF File Creation in Microsoft Word.

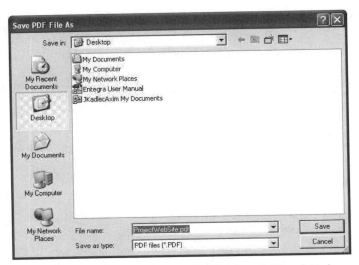

Figure 5.9: Central Project Information — PDF File Save Screen in Microsoft Word.

Once you are comfortable with Microsoft Word's capabilities to create an HTML page or PDF file, the next logical step is to graduate to Microsoft FrontPage, which has additional Graphical User Interface (GUI) web design capabilities. If you are a seasoned programmer, feel free to develop a site with ASP (Active Server Pages) or ColdFusion, or leverage any of the .NET Framework technologies to build a web site for the project.

A final option that has been recently introduced by Microsoft is the SharePoint technologies, such as Team Services and Portal Server. You can quickly create a functional web site with drag-and-drop capabilities by using Web Parts. For information about SharePoint products and Web Parts, see http://www. microsoft.com/sharepoint/ or *The Rational Guide To Building SharePoint Web Parts*, available at www.rationalpress.com.

Table 5.4 shows an example web page for the SQL Server 2000 Upgrade project. The top portion of the page allows Stakeholders, Executives and Management to obtain high level information for the project at a glance. Since Stakeholders have limited amounts of time, encourage them to visit the web site on a regular basis for two to three minutes to quickly track progress and contact the Project Manager with any questions.

SQL Server 6.5 to 2000 Upgrade – Project Web Site	
Project Status	On Schedule
Percentage Complete	23%
Freeze Date	11.18.2002
Upgrade Date	12.20.2002
Thaw Date	12.26.2002
Most Critical Issue	Pooling Budgets for the Project
Project Manager	Ted	X1199	ted@company.com
Meeting Day, Time and Location	Thursday's @ 10:00 AM ET – Potomac Room
Conference Call Number	888.888.8888 Pass Code 12345

KEY PROJECT DOCUMENTS
- Project Plan   ☒ ☒

PHASE DOCUMENTS	
• Project Scope	• Roles and Responsibilities
• Requirements Analysis	
• Functional Testing Plan	• Functional Testing Exceptions
• End User Testing Plan – Coming Soon!	• Load Testing Plan – Coming Soon!
• Upgrade Checklist	• Post Mortem Survey

UPGRADE LINKS
- How to Upgrade SQL Server 6.5 and 7.0 to SQL Server 2000
- How to move a SQL Server Database – SQL ServerCentral.com
Last Updated 11.07.2002 1:30 PM ET

Table 5.4: Central Project Information — Sample Project Web Site.

Table 5.4 shows the main features of the project web site:

▶ **Project Status and Percentage Complete Fields** — A single indicator that is color coded to identify the overall status of the project (Green = "On Schedule;" Yellow = "Slightly Behind Schedule;" Red = "Behind Schedule").

▶ **Critical Project Dates** — Freeze (final code release date), Upgrade (implementation date) and Thaw (new code release date).

▶ **Project Manager Information** — Identifies the Project Manager, with associated contact information for easy access.

▶ **Meeting Information** — Provides a quick reference about the date, time, and location for the next meeting, and any conference call numbers, if applicable.

▶ **Key Project Documents** — Includes the Project Plan, Issues List and Meeting Information. These documents are updated on a regular basis as the project progresses.

▶ **Phase Documents** — Includes the technical documents that support the project.

▶ **Upgrade Links** — Internal or external documents to supplement the project.

▶ **Update Time Stamp** — The web page is completed with the update date/time stamp.

Keeping the Project on Track

Communication is an integral component of Project Management that significantly impacts its success. As the Project Manager, you need to keep the team excited about the project and not neglect any team member. Meet regularly, both on a formal and informal basis, to ensure communication is free-flowing. If you have a geographically dispersed team, take the time to meet with the team members at critical points in the project and leverage technology to shorten the distances. Finally, ensure that all project documents are current and accurately reflect the project. These simple steps will go a long way to ensure the success of the project.

Lessons Learned

▶ Communication is a key component of successful Project Management that cannot be overlooked and must be addressed and leveraged during every interaction among the team members.

▶ Establish an Issues List to determine the potential project problems and assign a single task to a single team member for timely correction.

▶ Define the Roles and Responsibilities. Clearly identify the Project Roles with the associated Responsibilities, and assign at least one team member to the Role to complement the Project Plan. Everyone must know what they are supposed to do.

▶ Leverage the Meeting Agenda and Minutes to properly manage and record important information from all project meetings.

▶ Sign-Off should complete each phase of the Project Plan to ensure approval from the Stakeholders. This can be easily completed via email in Outlook.

▶ To facilitate communication among team members, avoid version control problems and prevent flooded email servers, set up a Centralized Project Information store that the entire team can review.

FREE

Bonus:

Sample Sign-Off email communications are available as free downloads when you register your book at www.rationalpress.com.

Part II

Working With Teams

RATIONAL PRESS

Chapter 6

Kick Off Meeting

"A journey of a thousand miles starts with a single step."
- Proverb

Pre-Meeting Preparations

Now that the Stakeholders have identified the Project Scope and first revisions of the Project and Communication Plans have been created, the Kick-Off meeting is the first opportunity to meet, review these documents, and obtain consensus from the entire team. As the Project Manager, it is necessary to achieve three personal goals for a successful Kick-Off meeting:

▶ Start momentum for the project with the entire team.

▶ Start the entire team on a positive note and make sure everyone is on the same page.

▶ Get the entire team excited about the project as a benefit the organization.

One tip for both the Kick-Off meeting and the remainder of the project meetings is to see if someone on the team will take notes for the meetings. Whenever possible, I always ask someone to take minutes for me so I can concentrate on the meeting and address any comments, questions or concerns. If I do not have this luxury, I end up frantically scribbling notes while trying to conduct the meeting. My end result is a few sheets of paper that are hard to decipher and I end up relying on my memory for some of the important details. Needless to say, this very quickly becomes nerve-wracking and can easily be corrected by the assistance of another team member.

Another tip is to give adequate advance notice to team members via email. This may be a day or two in some companies and a week in others. At times, the information pertaining to the project does not always trickle down to everyone on the team. Be sure to follow up with the Stakeholders to ensure they have notified their team or use this as an opportunity to either meet or catch up with each individual.

Kick-Off Meeting

With your goals well-established, set up a 60-minute Kick-Off meeting that includes Users, Stakeholders, Developers, Network Administrators, Testers and DBAs. In this meeting, it is necessary for the entire team to agree on and/or refine the project goals outlined in the Project Scope, as well as obtain commitments with consensus on the Project Plan contents. The Meeting Agenda should consist of the following items:

▶ Review the Project Scope, including Vision, Goals, Feasibility Analysis and Cost-Benefit Analysis.

▶ Review the Project Plan in detail, including proposed project phases; determine acceptable time frames and assign resources to individual tasks.

▶ Review the Communication Plan:

- Review Roles and Responsibilities and validate that the information is accurate and can be assigned to team members.

- Notify the team of the centralized web site and indicate the schedule of when the contents will be updated.

- Talk about Sign-Off at the end of each phase and ensure that it will be completed via email with **Approve** and **Reject** voting buttons.

- Notify the team of project documentation (such as the Issues List and Meeting Information) and the purpose for the documentation.

- Notify the team of phase documentation and use the example of the Project Scope Document.

▶ Provide an opportunity for any team member to address any item which has not been covered but is critical to the project.

▶ Provide contact information to the group and encourage them to contact you with any comments, questions or concerns.

▶ Thank everyone for attending the meeting, for their on-going contributions to the project, and end the meeting on time and on a positive note.

Post Meeting

Following the meeting, be sure to promptly update all project documents, including the Meeting Minutes and Issues List, post the documents on the project web site and send a reminder email (with the appropriate URL) to the group, telling them that the documents have been updated.

Lessons Learned

▶ Consider the Kick-Off meeting as the first opportunity to meet with your entire team to start the project on a positive note.

▶ Get the team excited about the project and build momentum.

▶ In this meeting, work toward commitments with consensus among the team.

FREE

Bonus:

A sample Meeting Agenda Minutes document is available as a free download when you register your book at www.rationalpress.com.

Chapter 7

Requirements Analysis

"The greatest of all faults, I should say, is to be conscious of none."
—Thomas Carlyle

The Requirements Analysis is the process of determining the needs for the entire project life cycle including Maintenance. Conduct the Analysis at the start of the project so that platform issues can be correctly addressed and not become resource hogs over time. The details from the Project Scope should be refined to determine the project's needs versus wants, and to determine the implementation schedule. It is necessary to have the entire team participate in the Requirements Analysis and review the major revisions for agreement and accuracy. Take the time to complete the Requirements Analysis correctly so that the end product can benefit the organization on the first delivery. Do not rush the process. Ensure that the key individuals are engaged in building a high-quality set of information.

I am certain that many people have horror stories related to inaccurate project requirements which led to over-budget projects with missed deadlines and irate Stakeholders. Heed my warning: it is imperative to thoroughly complete the Requirements Analysis, leaving no stone unturned. In the short term, it will take time to complete this phase, but in the long term, everyone related to the project will reap the benefits of the time spent.

As you start any project, be prepared for the requirements to change in varying degrees. To be proactive, determine your available options as soon as possible to make a final decision and prevent future changes. These options can be incorporated in the Requirements Analysis with the final decision. On a more reactive basis, Stakeholders or team members may indicate that requirements need to change. In these situations, properly assess each situation and determine the impact. As the Project Manager, do not be afraid to return to this stage in the project to verify and test. Do not let a change or oversight cause long-term problems for the project.

Figure 7.1 shows the SQL Server 2000 Requirements Analysis Project Plan tasks.

	❶	Task Name	Duration	Start	Finish	Prede	% omplet	Resource Names
1		⊟ SQL Server 6.5 to 2000 Upgrade	40 days	Mon 11/4/02	Fri 12/27/02		0%	
2		⊞ Project Scope	4 days	Mon 11/4/02	Thu 11/7/02		0%	
9		⊟ Requirements Analysis	7 days	Fri 11/8/02	Mon 11/18/02	2	0%	
10		Kick Off Meeting	1 day	Fri 11/8/02	Fri 11/8/02		0%	Project Manager
11		Identify, Order and Obtain Hardware	7 days	Fri 11/8/02	Mon 11/18/02		0%	Network Admin
12	📖	Develop Test Plans	7 days	Fri 11/8/02	Mon 11/18/02		0%	Tester
13		SQL Server Configurations and Security	7 days	Fri 11/8/02	Mon 11/18/02		0%	DBA
14	📖	Determine Communication Procedure	1 day	Fri 11/8/02	Fri 11/8/02		0%	Project Manager
15	📖	Complete Requirements Analysis	7 days	Fri 11/8/02	Mon 11/18/02		0%	Project Manager
16	📖	Requirements Analysis Sign-Off	0 days	Mon 11/18/02	Mon 11/18/02	15	0%	Stakeholders
17		⊞ Test Environment Setup	5 days	Tue 11/19/02	Mon 11/25/02	9	0%	

Figure 7.1: Project Plan — Requirements Analysis Tasks.

Writing the Requirements Analysis

The key to writing the Requirements Analysis document is to start with basic information and expand to greater detail, similar to what we did for the Project Plan. If team members are having a difficult time providing input, use the questionnaire in Table 7.2 to gather information. Write down what you think the requirements are, based on the gathered information. Have the team make comments on the document. At times, getting information on paper is difficult and the team members may work more efficiently with a document they can review, rather than starting from scratch.

Be prepared to write at least three to five major revisions based on feedback you receive. In addition, use examples and graphics related to the project to best illustrate your points. Finally, it is recommended to leverage existing documents and link to these documents to have a modular set of information. By doing so, you will only need to update a single document, preventing conflicting information from confusing the project team members.

On one particular development project, my goal was to work with Project Stakeholders and key members on the Requirements Analysis, but it was not productive. It was difficult to find a time when everyone could meet and asking everyone to prepare general information for a meeting yielded nothing. After a few days of going nowhere, I decided to write the high-level Requirements and distributed the information via email to obtain feedback. I was able to obtain feedback from most team members and met with others individually, despite scheduling conflicts. Since this project, I have always written the first revision of the Requirements Analysis in order to prevent these early problems and streamline the process.

The SQL Server 2000 Upgrade Requirements Analysis document is shown in Table 7.1.

SQL SERVER 6.5 TO 2000 UPGRADE – REQUIREMENTS ANALYSIS

PROJECT GOALS

- Meet all deadlines as prescribed in the Project Plan.
- Upgrade with better performance than the SQL Server 6.5 environment.
- Minimize the downtime needed for the upgrade.
- Establish free-flowing communication to enable the team to work closely.
- Have the project serve as a test bed for future projects with a similar format.

PROJECT BUDGET

- Pooled budget from the Operations and IT budget will pay for the hardware, software and project team salary and expenses.

KEY PROJECT DATES

- Project completion should be in a two month time frame from the start date.
- Freeze Date – 11.18.2002.
- Upgrade Date – 12.20.2002.
- Thaw Date – 12.26.2002.

MEETINGS

KEY PROJECT DOCUMENTS

Project Plan	Task, resource and due date to complete the project
Issues List	All problems and potential problems recorded by date, with an assigned individual responsible for addressing the issue
Agenda and Minutes	Proposed meeting items, decisions and attendees
Project Scope	High level project goals and boundaries
Roles and Responsibilities	Project roles and assigned responsibilities
Upgrade Checklist	Detailed steps for the SQL Server 6.5 to 2000 Upgrade
Coding Re-Design	Techniques to improve
Functional Testing Plan	Test plan to compare the applications in SQL Server 6.5 and 2000 to ensure all needed capabilities are available
End User Testing Plan	User plan to verify acceptable application performance
Load Testing Plan	Test plan to determine the SQL Server Capacity under stress
Testing Exceptions	Detailed record of testing problems and associated corrections
Lessons Learned Survey	Project completion information on a per individual basis

Table 7.1: Core Project Document — Requirements Analysis.

SQL SERVER 6.5 TO 2000 UPGRADE – REQUIREMENTS ANALYSIS

PROJECT TEAM
- See the Roles and Responsibilities document for the team member details.
- In order to complete the project, we need an expert on the SQL Server 2000 Upgrade process (due to the limited number of available resources).

PROJECT HARDWARE
- A new production server will be recommended by Networking and DBAs.
- Existing Development and Test Servers will be leveraged.
- All ☒indows and SQL Server licensing are included in the Enterprise Licensing Agreement from Microsoft.

TESTING
- The Functional, End User and Load Testing will be formalized via a test plan.
- All problematic results will be recorded on the correct Exceptions Document.

TECHNICAL REQUIREMENTS
- Overall system performance should be better than the SQL Server 6.5 environment.
- Data should be archived on a quarterly basis.
- Security should be improved and all Users should authenticate via ☒indows Authentication.
- System should be available Monday through Saturday from 7:00 AM to 12:00 AM ET. A fault tolerant architecture should prevent a catastrophic event from causing extended downtime.

ADDITIONAL ITEMS
- Review the project documents for additional requirements, specifications and project decisions.
- Sign-Off will be necessary at the completion of each phase of the project.

Table 7.1: Core Project Document — Requirements Analysis (continued).

Requirements Analysis Questionnaire

Asking the appropriate questions to obtain the necessary information for the Requirements Analysis phase is key to the overall success of the project. Although no single set of questions can be created to meet all requirements for all projects, Table 7.2 provides a sample set of questions in the form of a questionnaire that could be used as a template for most projects and could be supplemented with project-specific questions.

REQUIREMENTS ANALYSIS QUESTIONNAIRE		
GENERAL INFORMATION		
Project Name		
Project Stakeholders		
Project Team Members		
Project Manager		
PROJECT GOALS		
ID	**QUESTION**	**ANSWER**
1	☒hat are the project goals?	
2	☒hat business benefits will the project satisfy?	
3	☒hat are the absolute needs versus wants for the project?	
4	Are other projects or business initiatives going to impact this project?	
5	Do any other projects have inputs to this project which make it a dependency?	
6	Does this project serve as input to any other projects and subsequently delay those projects?.	
7	Does the Feasibility Analysis require any updates?	
8	☒hat are the policies and standards that apply to this project?	
9	Does any legislation or regulations impact this project?	
TECHNICAL ASPECTS		
ID	**QUESTION**	**ANSWER**
1	Is there a product/process in the marketplace that will resolve the problem or do we need to build the product/process in house?	
2	☒hat are the hardware and software needs for development and testing?	
3	☒hat are the hardware and software needs for the production platform?	
4	☒hat are the testing requirements?	

Table 7.2: Core Project Document — Requirements Analysis Questionnaire.

	REQUIREMENTS ANALYSIS QUESTIONNAIRE	
5	⊠hat are the performance requirements for response time?	
6	⊠hat are the uptime requirements for fault tolerance or redundancy?	
7	⊠hat are the long term support needs from an operational and maintenance perspective?	
8	⊠hat additional aspects should be taken into consideration?	
TIME FRAME		
ID	**QUESTION**	**ANSWER**
1	⊠hat are the key dates (start, freeze, implementation, thaw, completion) for the project?	
2	Are we dependent on any hardware or software releases from a third party to complete the project?	
3	Does any equipment need to be ordered that could delay the project?	
BUDGET		
ID	**QUESTION**	**ANSWER**
1	⊠hat project budget is available?	
2	Can any of the development expense for the project be capitalized?	
3	Does the Cost Benefit Analysis require any updates?	
PROJECT TEAM AVAILABILITY		
ID	**QUESTION**	**ANSWER**
1	⊠ho are the key team members and which skills are valuable?	
2	Are skills required to complete the project tasks that are not available from any existing team member? Do we need to hire new employees, train existing employees or partner with a technical services company?	

Table 7.2: Core Project Document — Requirements Analysis Questionnaire (continued).

I started using a questionnaire on a large infrastructure project. I actually sent it to everyone on the team, who happened to be in a few different locations. I suspected that the team was not on the same page, so I used the questionnaire as an eye-opening tool to let everyone on the team know what the rest of the team was thinking. Based on the information, we were able to come to terms on the needs for the project.

On an informal side note, I typically generate key questions to gather necessary information for the project requirements. I use the questionnaire as a general guide to gather information to compile the first revision of the Requirements

Analysis. I recommend taking the time to build a small set of questions, to think about areas of the project that may be of great concern in the short or long term.

Requirements Analysis Completion

It is necessary to document the requirements for the project and not deviate from these items nor add items over the course of the project once Sign-Off is obtained. Unfortunately, this is easier said than done. If items are deviated from or added to, my recommendation is to return to this phase of the project to rework the remainder of the phases. Too often, new requirements are added and considered minimal, when in fact these changes have a ripple effect on the project, causing rework and missed deadlines. Be aware of this pitfall and work diligently to have a comprehensive set of requirements to prevent this problem. When it does occur, notify the team promptly of the changes and quantify the impact with time and budgetary figures. If earlier stages of the project are reworked, be sure to incorporate the updated Sign-Off.

Lessons Learned

▶ Assemble the first revision of the Requirements Analysis to work toward a comprehensive set of Requirements.

▶ To gather the Project Requirements, assemble a questionnaire to obtain information from the Stakeholders and key team members.

▶ If a team member requires significant changes to the Requirements Analysis, do not be afraid to return to the this phase to ensure the project is properly completed.

Chapter 8

Working With Difficult Team Members

"Teamwork is neither 'good' nor 'desirable.' It is a fact. Wherever people work together or play together, they do so as a team. Which team to use for what purpose is a crucial, difficult and risky decision that is even harder to unmake."
—Peter F. Drucker

One of the key skills identified at the start of the book that Project Managers need is Personnel Management. It is an absolute necessity. The Communication Plan should serve as a foundation for working with and as part of a team. By this phase, even though these plans are in place and the project has been approved as part of the Requirements Analysis Sign-Off, it is necessary to discuss working with difficult team members. Under deadlines, it may be necessary to leverage techniques typically used outside the scope of the Communication Plan.

Techniques for Team Building

Communication expectations should have been properly set with the Project Scope, Project Plan, Requirements Analysis and Communication Plan. Most of the time, these documents do their job and you need only work with a person or two to sync them with the remainder of the team. The end goal is to find a common bond for success! This can be accomplished in a number of different ways and each circumstance will require a different approach.

One of the easiest and most overlooked techniques to solve a problem is to meet one-on-one with the individual over lunch or a drink outside of the office to determine the root problem. During this time, it is necessary to be "other" focused to satisfy this individual's needs. By "other focused," I mean that you should listen to what they have to say and not jump to conclusions. Work with the individual and answer all their questions. Once this is accomplished, verify the message to ensure you understand the actual problem. Once this is understood, correct the behavior, not the personality. Use persuasion rather than authority to assimilate the person into the group. Build a small and informal plan to give the individual ownership in the project. This will help the person be a 'winner' and feel like they have made a contribution to the project.

Along the same lines, it is necessary to continue to build a strong relationship with the entire team. It is not a good idea to sacrifice an individual for the team. As such, it is always a good idea to have lunches or a happy hour with the entire team on a regular basis to relax outside of work. Build that trust. Typically, these interactions strengthen the personal relationships necessary for a unified team over the course of current and future projects.

As more companies are opening offices around the world, working with geographically dispersed teams can make completing projects more challenging. Generally, it is more difficult to communicate via phone and email as opposed to in-person interactions. At times, Project Managers experience rivalry and control problems between sites, as well as resistance to work with someone from another site. I believe in healthy competition, but if this is taken to an extreme, it is detrimental to the overall project. One technique to address this problem is to schedule a visit to all team member sites. By planning ahead, the costs could be minimal and the time to build a relationship with the team members at the remote site can reap benefits, not only for the current project, but for future projects.

I try to make these trips a priority and budget time and travel costs into the overall project investment. I prefer to schedule these trips on a monthly basis to have face time with the entire team or a team member. These trips are intended to spend time addressing major issues, brainstorming for needed resolutions, and so on. I also try to meet with everyone on an individual basis to discuss the future steps in the project and ensure their buy-in for the upcoming work. Finally, I also make it a point to have lunch and dinner meetings, not only to discuss items related to the project, but also to enjoy good times with good people!

Are People Holding Back?

If Project Management is new to your organization, one common problem Project Managers face is team members holding back information or ideas. Generally, this is because they think their thoughts will not make much of a difference, or that they are offering only a little detail that can be addressed later. These little details can mean all the success in the world to the project, and you need to remind your team that this is the case. For the Stakeholders, remind them that complete and accurate information is needed to mitigate risk, and that this will ultimately achieve project success.

Another common problem is that team members do not speak up about potential problems or concerns. This is especially prevalent during status meetings where the entire team is on the call. At times, people feel uncomfortable about talking in front of a group, where one comment can spark an idea from another team member.

To resolve these problems, be approachable and set an honest example as the Project Manager. Ask the group if they have additional feedback and make eye contact with everyone in the room or ask people individually on the call. If you sense hesitation, let the team member know and ask for more feedback. Typically, this invitation will solicit a response that can be addressed by the team. If this is not the case, use silence to elicit a response. Silence in most cases makes people uncomfortable and if you are willing to wait 10 to 15 seconds for a response, you will hear the comments, questions and concerns. At the conclusion of the meeting, end the meeting on a positive note by thanking everyone for their time and voice your contact information to encourage them to stop by your office or send an email with any issues prior to the next status meeting.

Are People NOT Holding Back?

"A cynic is a man who knows the price of everything and the value of nothing." – Oscar Wilde

For as many times as people hold back information, you will be faced with "Bullies," "Jokers" and "Cynics" in the course of completing a project. Although I am not a behavioral specialist or psychologist, I want to provide some suggestions to address this common problem. When you are faced with a person who has one of these dispositions, you need to address this mind-set in a much different manner than in the previously mentioned case.

When you have to work with a "Bully," "Joker" or "Cynic," it is necessary to acknowledge all of their needs, but do not let them take over the meeting, cause problems for the overall team progress, or halt momentum. It is easy to see that these three outcomes are destructive to the overall project. The Project Manager needs to address these items quickly to prevent project-long problems.

Heed the person's comments, understand their viewpoint, but stay the course. Ignore any temper tantrums or anxiety attacks, because it is typically not in one's best interest to engage a person in that emotional state. Typically, the person wants to fight and gets pleasure from fighting or is looking for attention. Most bullies do not like being ignored, but by doing so you are not giving them anything to fight and thereby deflating their balloon.

In real time, ensure that you have "dotted all of your i's and cross all your t's" for the items the individual is contending. If you are wrong, it is easier to concede and correct the problem before the person tries to make the proverbial "mountain out of a mole hill." If not, and you are comfortable addressing the item, use only logic and facts to systematically defeat the points. Do not insult the person. Most bullies do not like logic and feed off of emotion in order to fight.

The next day, meet one-on-one with the person in an informal manner and let them know how detrimental their behavior is to the project. Make sure it is addressed promptly, and only after emotions have subsided. Prepare the needed information that will allow the individual to ultimately make positive contributions to the team. I do not recommend meeting with the person in a confrontational manner, but in a constructive manner. Do not fall victim to 'fight fire with fire' unless absolutely necessary. Typically, this tactic is one that cannot be undone. Your goal is to work to assimilate the person into the team. This will not be a simple task, and it will take significant time and energy. Good luck!

Final Options

The previous sections are generally very beneficial when working with an individual team member who becomes challenging. Unfortunately, these techniques sometimes do not resolve the problem, which may persist or even become worse. During these instances, you need to use the tactics outlined in this section as a last resort to solve the problems for the sake of the project. Unfortunately, some behavior is simply unacceptable, such as "road blocking," incessant fighting and using profane language. These problems need to be addressed properly and quickly. They should not be catered to, because the problems will only fester. In these circumstances, take the bull by the horns for the sake of the project.

When major problems are occurring between members of the team, you have to keep in mind that you are the Project Manager and you are ultimately responsible for the success or failure of the project. Since you are in this position, you need to stick your neck out and don't be 'Mr. Nice Guy!' It is necessary to look for other options to solve the problem. If you must, go above or around the person that is causing the problem. You may have to be creative, but there are few problems that do not have alternatives. If you are not very familiar with the individual, speak with the appropriate Management and explain the situation and the course of action already taken. Ask for suggestions for resolving the problem. As a final option, notify the team member that you are seeking Human Resource disciplinary action to resolve the problem and follow through with the steps to have the individual removed from the team or organization, if absolutely necessary.

Lessons Learned

▶ Working with Team Members can be one of the most challenging components of a Project. It is important to build a bond among team members.

▶ Be sure to probe for proper information, because small details can create a domino effect that can cause major delays and rework for the entire project.

▶ Remember that as the Project Manager you are ultimately responsible for the success of the project and need to take the necessary measures to ensure success.

Design,
Development
and Delivery

Chapter 9

Design, Development and Baseline Testing

"Quality is never an accident, it is always the result of an intelligent effort."
— John Ruskin

When faced with building or integrating a product in your environment or developing a process for an IT project, it is necessary to focus on quality from the onset of design and development. The quality focus should be applied as an iterative approach to Design, Development and Testing to quickly and accurately deliver the needed solution. Also, think about the long-term design and development, because with an iterative model, the foundation should be able to easily incorporate the next set of functionality. Think of this like the construction of a home: you must build the first story of a home properly on top of the foundation. All of the piping and electrical work needs to be properly designed to apply the fixtures once the walls are assembled. Remember the long-term goals. If the initial design is hasty, a great deal of reworking could be necessary later. Try to prepare yourself as a marathon runner for the design process and as a sprinter for the development process. The combination of these mindsets should yield the desired results.

Once you are in the right state of mind, write the Design Document by starting small and growing to meet the long-term vision. Then begin to develop the process or technology which meets the project requirements. In both design and development, you must address the core items first and then expand with additional items in a modular fashion. This premise can easily be applied to your database entity relationship diagram (ERD) as well as your object model for the middle tier and front end code. One of the most prevalent trends today is related to scalability. Make sure the architecture is scalable for easy enhancements and upgrades, and ensure that necessary standards are set and followed to consistently complete the project.

As the tasks from the design and development section of the Project Plan are being completed, it is necessary from a Developer perspective to conduct baseline testing as a part of this iterative phase. The goal of the baseline testing is to generally validate the design and development work. The testing at this phase in the project is conducted on more of an individual basis; the Developer should head this work with a few key Users to ensure that the application meets existing requirements.

One of the greatest lessons I have learned regarding Application Development projects is to get the application into the hands of the users as quickly as possible. I have found that frequent meetings yielded the most valuable feedback in terms of accuracy, efficiency and reasonable enhancements. It is amazing to see how Users "light up" when they see the application and feel a sense of ownership when their feedback is directly incorporated. I am not referring to major code re-writes, but simple recommendations about color suggestions and layout on the screen as it relates to daily work flows for greater productivity.

Another valuable lesson that I want to share is about incorporating a pilot phase in the project, whereby the application or process is released to a small set of Users to use it to meet business needs for a period of time. A similar principle can be used with third-party applications, where my recommendation is to get the product in-house as soon as possible to determine if the product meets the needs. Most vendors will comply with this request and may even work with you on a baseline installation to expand to the entire organization. The bottom line from all of this information is to start small and then expand.

Figure 9.1 breaks down the SQL Server 2000 Upgrade Design, Development and Baseline Testing Project Plan tasks to build the Upgrade process, test the process in a few scenarios and finalize the documentation to complete the process.

	o	Task Name	Duration	Start	Finish	Prede	% omplet	Resource Names
1		⊟ SQL Server 6.5 to 2000 Upgrade	40 days	Mon 11/4/02	Fri 12/27/02		0%	
2		⊞ Project Scope	4 days	Mon 11/4/02	Thu 11/7/02		0%	
9		⊞ Requirements Analysis	7 days	Fri 11/8/02	Mon 11/18/02	2	0%	
17		⊟ Test Environment Setup	5 days	Tue 11/19/02	Mon 11/25/02	9	0%	
18		Status Meeting	1 day	Tue 11/19/02	Tue 11/19/02		0%	Project Manager
19	🖫	Setup Hardware	5 days	Tue 11/19/02	Mon 11/25/02		0%	Network Admin,DBA,Tester
20		Test Environment Sign-Off	0 days	Mon 11/25/02	Mon 11/25/02	19	0%	Stakeholders
21		⊟ Preliminary Upgrade Testing	5 days	Tue 11/26/02	Mon 12/2/02	17	0%	
22		Status Meeting	1 day	Tue 11/26/02	Tue 11/26/02		0%	Project Manager
23	🖫	Design and Develop Upgrade Process	2 days	Tue 11/26/02	Wed 11/27/02		0%	DBA
24		Test Upgrade Process and Finalize Documentation	1 day	Thu 11/28/02	Thu 11/28/02	23	0%	DBA
25	🖫	Execute Preliminary Upgrade	1 day	Fri 11/29/02	Fri 11/29/02	24	0%	DBA
26	🖫	Preliminary Upgrade Exceptions Document	1 day	Mon 12/2/02	Mon 12/2/02	25	0%	DBA
27		Preliminary Upgrade Sign-Off	0 days	Mon 12/2/02	Mon 12/2/02	26	0%	Stakeholders
28		⊟ Production Environment Setup	5 days	Tue 11/26/02	Mon 12/2/02	17	0%	
29		Status Meeting	1 day	Tue 11/26/02	Tue 11/26/02		0%	Project Manager
30		Setup Hardware	5 days	Tue 11/26/02	Mon 12/2/02		0%	Network Admin,DBA
31		Production Environment Sign-Off	0 days	Mon 12/2/02	Mon 12/2/02	30	0%	Stakeholders
32		⊞ Functional Testing	7 days	Tue 12/3/02	Wed 12/11/02	31	0%	

Figure 9.1: Project Plan — Design, Development and Testing Project Plan Tasks.

Design, Development and Testing Specifications

The Design, Development and Testing phase takes on many faces depending on the type of project. During this phase, it is necessary to build a specification intended for an application development or infrastructure project. Specifications can vary, and no "one size fits all" approach can be recommended, nor can it serve as the norm. Make sure that the proper content and decision-making is incorporated to finalize the specification. A number of specifications that may be needed for IT Projects:

▶ Application Development Specification

- Software, Hardware, Front End, Middle Tier, DBMS, Screens, Workflows, etc.

▶ Design Specification

- Object Model, Data Model, Programming Language, etc.

▶ Reporting Suite

- Questions Requiring Answers, Delivery Mechanism, Reporting Cycle, Layout, etc.

▶ Version Control Process

- Check-out and Check-in Process, etc.

▶ Change Management Specification

- Rollout Process, Rollback Capabilities, Schedule, etc.

▶ Operations Support Guide

- Policies, Procedures, Standardization, Service Level Agreements, etc.

▶ Backup Plan

- Backup Frequency, Restore Process, Storage, etc.

▶ Maintenance Plans

- Type of Maintenance, Duration, Downtime, etc.

▶ Security Specification

- Network Security, Intrusion Detection, Encryption, etc.

▶ Disaster Recovery Plan

- Recovery Planning, Configuration Collection, Testing Scenarios, etc.

▶ High Availability Plan

- Up Time Requirements, Fail-Over Capacity, Acceptable Data Loss, etc.

▶ Implementation Plan\Integration Plan

- Date, Time, Task, Responsibility, Data Exchange, Connectivity, etc.

▶ Training Curriculum

- Material, Students, Testing, etc.

▶ Upgrade Specification

- Programming Specification, Upgrade Specification, etc.

SQL Server 2000 Upgrade Programming Specification

A number of the configurations between SQL Server 6.5 and 2000 are significantly different, and require new techniques to properly design, develop and support the platform. Table 9.1 outlines the SQL Server 2000 Programming Specification that the Developers and DBAs would follow to ensure that the SQL Server 2000 code is compliant and performing optimally.

ID	Item	SQL Server 6.5	SQL Server 2000	Additional Information
1	ANSI NULLS	• Default – ANSI NULLS is OFF	• Default – ANSI NULLS is ON	• Validate NULL comparisons are operating properly and ensure IS NULL and IS NOT NULL expressions are being used rather than =NULL or <> NULL
2	Quoted Identifiers	• Default – SET QUOTED_IDENTI-FIER OFF	• Default – SET QUOTED_IDENTIFIER ON	• Variables are denoted by single quotes in T-SQL code • Keywords are denoted by double quotes in T-SQL mode • See the SET QUOTED_IDENTIFIER article in Books Online
3	SQL Server Keywords	• Basic list of Keywords	• Expanded list of Keywords	• Ensure object names are not SQL Server Keywords or rely on the Quoted Identifiers
4	System Objects	• Baseline set of objects	• More System Tables, Views, Stored Procedures and Functions • Introduction of ANSI Views to query data	• Pay close attention to code directly accessing system tables and migrate to use stored procedures and INFORMATION-SCHEMA Views
5	JOIN Types	• ANSI syntax with ⊠HERE clause comparison	• ANSI JOIN syntax (INNER, OUTER, FULL and CROSS)	• See the 'Types of Joins' article in Books Online for additional details
6	Query Plans	• Default – LOOP	• HASH • MERGE • NESTED LOOP	• See the 'Understanding Hash Joins', Understanding Merge Joins', 'Understanding Nested Loops Joins', articles in Books Online for additional details
7	Data Exchange	• BCP • Bulk Insert	• XML (Extensible Markup Language) • DTS (Data Transformation Services)	• XML – Ability to ubiquitously transfer data among heterogeneous systems • DTS – Extraction, Transformation and Load programming tool
8	Data access	• Cursors-based processing	• Set based data access • TABLE Data Type • User Defined Functions • SELECT TOP clause	• Improved ability to deliver data by more efficient means
9	Reporting	• Reporting from Operational Systems	• Analysis Services • Data Mining Algorithms	• See '⊠hat's New in Analysis Services' article in Books Online • See 'Data Mining Enhancements' article in Books Online

Table 9.1: Design Specification — SQL Server 2000 Upgrade Programming Considerations.

SQL Server 2000 Upgrade Implementation Checklist

Another specification needed during the SQL Server 2000 Upgrade that is developed during the Design, Development and Testing Phase is the Upgrade Implementation Checklist. During this phase, the DBAs would work with the Developers, Network Administrators and Testing staff to determine the proper steps to adhere to during the Preliminary Upgrade for Testing purposes and the Production Upgrade. This specification, shown in Figure 9.2, documents the task name, instructions, location where the work should be completed, and who is responsible for completing the task. In effect, this checklist becomes a plan itself, which the staff can use at the console during the Upgrade.

ID	Task	Directions	Server	Responsibility
1	Verify the SQL Server Service PACK is SQL Server 6.5 Service Pack 5a	• T-SQL – SELECT @@VERSION	SQL 6.5 Prod	DBA
2	Verify the SQL Server Internal Name	• T-SQL – SELECT @@USERNAME • Output – Machine Name	SQL 6.5 Prod	DBA
3	Set User Databases to Read-Only Mode	• T-SQL – USE master EXEC sp_dboption 'database_name', 'read only', "TRUE"	SQL 6.5 Prod	DBA
4	Execute DBCC's to verify databases are free of consistency and allocation errors	• T-SQL – DBCC CHECKDB, NE⊠ALLOC, TEXTALLOC and CHECKCATALOG • Verify no error messages are recorded in the output	SQL 6.5 Prod	DBA
5	Generate Object Scripts	• Enterprise Manager – Execute the Generate Scripts application and record all objects in the script	SQL 6.5 Prod	DBA
6	Record the SQL Server Scheduled Tasks	• Enterprise Manager – SQL Server Executive Jobs	SQL 6.5 Prod	DBA
7	Record SQL Server Configurations	• T-SQL – Save the results of Sp_configure to a text file • General – Record any other Server, SQL Server or application configurations	SQL 6.5 Prod	DBA
8	Verify the System Error Logs	• Enterprise Manager – Review the SQL Server Error Log for any errors • Event Log – Review the System, Application and Security Logs	SQL 6.5 Prod	DBA
9	Set SQL Server Executive to Manual and Stop the Service	• Enterprise Manager	SQL 6.5 Prod	DBA
10	Change Machine Name and IP	• ⊠indows Tools	SQL 6.5 Prod	Network Admin
11	Record Table Row Counts	• T-SQL – SELECT statements or sp_spaceused	SQL 6.5 Prod	DBA
12	Backup System and User Databases as 'sa'	• T-SQL – DUMP DATABASE	SQL 6.5 Prod	DBA

Table 9.2: Redundant Upgrade Architecture — SQL Server 2000 Upgrade Checklist.

ID	Task	Directions	Server	Responsibility
13	BCP syslogins from the SQL 6.5 Prod to the Upgrade Server	• DOS – BCP Command	SQL 6.5 Prod	DBA
14	Remove Server from the Network	• ⊠indows – Shutdown	SQL 6.5 Prod	Network Admin
15	Ensure TempOB in 3 Fold the OLTP TempDB size as well as Master and MSDB have free space	• T-SQL – ALTER DATABASE	Upgrade Server	DBA
16	Create the Devices/Databases	• T-SQL – DISK INT, CREATE DATABASE	Upgrade Server	DBA
17	Load the User Databases as 'sa'	• T-SQL – LOAD Database	Upgrade Server	DBA
18	Execute the Pipeline Upgrade ⊠izard	• SQL Server Upgrade ⊠izard • Named Pipe, Successful Object Data Transfer and Exhaustive Data Transfer • Code Page, ANSI NULLS, and Quoted identifiers Settings	Upgrade Server	DBA
19	Review the Upgrade Output	• Differences Report • *.err and *.out Files	Upgrade Server	DBA
20	Compare Row Counts	• T-SQL – SELECT statements or sp_helpindex	Upgrade Server/ SQL 6.5 Prod	DBA
21	Execute Backup and Restore operations as 'sa'	• T-SQL – BACKUP DATABASE • T-SQL – RESTORE DATABASE	Upgrade Server/ SQL 2K Prod	DBA
22	Migrate SQL Server Jobs and Logins	• T-SQL – sp_addjob • T-SQL – BCP Command	Upgrade Server/ SQL 2K Prod	DBA
23	Execute UPDATE STATISTICS	• T-SQL – UPDATE STATISTICS	SQL 2K Prod	DBA
24	Execute Functional Application Testing	• Business Applications	SQL 2K Prod	Testers
25	Monitor Production Environment, Configure and Tune SQL Server	• SQL Server Profiler • ⊠indows System Monitor • T-SQL – System Stored Procedures	SQL 2K Prod	DBA

Table 9.2: Redundant Upgrade Architecture — SQL Server 2000 Upgrade Checklist (continued).

Lessons Learned

▶ Work diligently to get the application in the hands of the users ASAP to obtain immediate feedback and guide the remainder of the phase.

▶ Design, Development and Testing should be considered an iterative process, starting small with core functionality and expanding into a full-scale solution.

▶ Design, Development and Test specifications are practical and easy to use, yielding an accurate and efficient application or process to benefit the business.

Chapter 10

Curve Ball Prevention and Management

"On the whole human beings want to be good, but not too good and not quite all the time."
— George Orwell

The best way to manage project curve balls is by preventing them, or "nipping them in the bud." It is best to think about curve balls at the start of the project, and try to prevent them from happening by planning accordingly. I recommend identifying items at the start of the project that are outside of your control that could delay the project. A brainstorming session could be a very beneficial proactive approach, rather than being reactive at particular times in the project. In addition, some of the most detrimental curve balls are minor details that are overlooked but ultimately have a ripple effect through the rest of the project. In short, stay a step or two ahead of the problems to prevent yourself from falling victim to a curve ball.

On most of the projects I manage, I am working directly with the technology and I am aware of the technical nuisances. On the few projects where I am not 100% proficient with the technology, I always speak with the technical guru to learn about that piece of technology. This learned information can uncover curve balls. I often take the time to understand as much as possible about the technology to strategize about the dangers and address them early. These simple steps have prevented a small problem from developing into sustained problems.

Recommendations for Common Curve Balls

The following general recommendations should prevent the majority of the most common curve balls:

▶ **Ensure proper group representation in each phase of the project** — One problem I see time and again is lack of representation from the Reporting groups. For some reason, Reporting is overlooked and it then becomes a major issue with Stakeholders when they do not receive critical reports necessary for decision making.

▶ **Manage the items on the Issues List to "Closed" Status** — The Issues List is a great source of information that cannot be overlooked. Identifying the Issue is half the battle; the Issue must be resolved and verified by you, the Project Manager, before the project can continue.

▶ **Communicate properly with the Team and Stakeholders** — It is especially important to make sure the Stakeholders are well informed. Be sure to stop by their office on a regular basis to ensure that the Stakeholders continue to fully support the project. This is a simple, common-sense step that can yield hours of savings.

▶ **Heed warnings from the various team members concerning multiple related items that are not on the Project Plan** — Discuss the items with the entire team in order to completely understand them. Put contingencies in place as steps in the project plan to mitigate associated risks and to prevent known problems.

▶ **Determine the differences in Project Scope and Requirements Analysis versus the actual status of the project** — Double check to ensure that you are meeting all of the project requirements and that the Stakeholders are pleased with the results.

▶ **Encourage Team members to freely voice their concerns** — Open communication should prevent a bubble from bursting that ends up on everyone's face as a major embarrassment.

▶ **Take the time to think about the situation and the appropriate answer** — You do not always have to provide an immediate answer. If you are providing real-time answers +90% of the time, you are doing very well. If you legitimately do not have an answer, concede and quickly find the answer.

▶ **Respond to the person with a solution request** — When someone brings an issue to your attention, ask for their recommendation. Most of the time, the person who raised the issue already has an answer and is looking for an audience to share the solution with. If this is not the case, a brainstorming session among the team can typically resolve the problem. Two heads are better than one, but many minds can deliver a solution!

▶ **Do not be afraid to ask questions to obtain additional information in circumstances where you do not understand the problem** — If you do not understand the implications of the problem, ask why the item is important to the project. This will help determine the appropriate course of action to resolve the problem.

Steps Toward Resolution

One common situation I am faced with on a regular basis is working with new individuals on projects that have tight deadlines and numerous requirements. If you are new to the environment, you might want to ask individuals internal and external to the team about issues they have experienced at the organization. Then find out how the items have been addressed. You will probably find that problems are similar between organizations and projects, but that each situation has its own nuisances that are specific to the organization.

When you are faced with a curve ball that has slipped through the cracks and needs to be promptly addressed, take some simple steps to address the item:

▶ Assess the severity of the problem and do not be caught in a situation where "elephants are running around and you are swatting at flies." Do not waste time and energy on items that do not have a high severity and do not have a high probability to occur.

▶ Conduct analysis to understand the problems and determine two to four alternatives.

▶ Determine the advantages and disadvantages of each alternative.

▶ Ascertain the appropriate Managerial Level notification among the team and among Stakeholders. Depending on the severity and probability, do not be afraid to raise the issue in order for the proper decision to be made in a timely manner.

▶ Plan, communicate, document and manage the implementation of the solution once the most appropriate course of action is selected.

One notorious curve ball to beware of is a person telling you that everything is going wrong or that "the sky is falling." I normally experience one of these situations per project, so be forewarned. Although the severity of the problem may be exaggerated, the problem is typically real and needs to be addressed. Following the steps described in this section may be very valuable in conjunction with a cool head and a clear picture of the problem.

Items Outside of My Control

What do you do when you are passed curve balls and the items are completely outside of your control? The reality is that some items are just that way, such as natural disasters, upper management's decisions or competing priorities. When faced with these items, assess the situation with respect to the entire environment. Depending on the item, determine other portions of the project that can be addressed in the short term and continue to make progress on the project. My best recommendation is to determine the available options and associated outcomes, then select the most appropriate course of action.

All of the problems I have faced have had an answer of some sort. It may not be the ideal answer, but I firmly believe that few situations have no options. If you are having a difficult time determining viable options, I recommend consulting others in your organization or some web research for an answer.

As a last resort, you can always 'punt' by adjusting the schedule if no alternatives are available in the short-term to resolve the problem as planned. Some examples that I have heard are related to natural disasters, the unexpected illness of a key team member, or family issues such as a death in the family. You cannot plan for every issue that may significantly impact the individual team members. Keep in mind that in the larger scheme of things, these items may be more important than the project. Respect the situation the fellow team member is experiencing and determine the necessary course of action to move forward.

Lessons Learned

▶ Curve balls and items outside of your control are a fact of Project Management, so take the time to think about potential curve balls and anticipate resolutions at the beginning of the project.

▶ When a curve ball or item outside of your control is thrown in your direction, take the time to assess the situation, determine two to four options, test the options, select the ideal option and implement it.

▶ If you are faced with catastrophic circumstances, and assessed the situation to be sure that no options are available, consider "punting" as a last resort, knowing that you can successfully achieve the project goals at a later date.

FREE *Bonus:*

Sample documents for the Project Scope, Project Plan, and Issues List are available as free downloads when you register your book at www.rationalpress.com.

Chapter 11

Formal Testing

"If everything seems to be going well, you have obviously overlooked something."
— *Steven Wright*

At this stage in the project, it is necessary to conduct formalized testing to finalize the project prior to the Implementation phase. Testing cannot be overemphasized, nor is it an area where corners can be cut. Having a fresh set of eyes to test and use the application can reap numerous benefits. I consider testing to be the most important checkpoint in the overall process to validate that the business needs are being met by the application or process. Unfortunately, testing has been undervalued in organizations, perhaps because they don't understand its benefits. A good Testing Team will push the limits of the application and use its valuable experiences to ensure that the application is going to release as few bugs as possible into the production environment. The Testing Team can also help determine the appropriate testing for the project. A number of applicable tests that are commonly performed prior to releasing an application or process are shown in Table 11.1.

ID	Test	Description	Responsibility
1	Baseline Testing in the Design, Development and Testing Phase	• Baseline testing to generally validate the application or process more from a programmatic perspective	• Developers • DBAs • Small User Group
2	Functional	• Validate that the application or process meets the project needs in the Requirements Analysis	• Testers
3	User Acceptance	• User validation of the application	• Users
4	Integration	• Verify the interoperability between other components in the environment	• Developers • DBAs • Network Administrators • Testers
5	Load	• Ensure the application performs well under high transaction levels	• Developers • DBAs • Testers

Table 11.1: Testing Options — Testing Overview.

	o	Task Name	Duration	Start	Finish	Predecessors	% Complete	Resource Names
1		⊟ SQL Server 6.5 to 2000 Upgrade	40 days	Mon 11/4/02	Fri 12/27/02		0%	
2		⊞ Project Scope	4 days	Mon 11/4/02	Thu 11/7/02		0%	
9		⊞ Requirements Analysis	7 days	Fri 11/8/02	Mon 11/18/02	2	0%	
17		⊞ Test Environment Setup	5 days	Tue 11/19/02	Mon 11/25/02	9	0%	
21		⊞ Preliminary Upgrade Testing	5 days	Tue 11/26/02	Mon 12/2/02	17	0%	
26		⊞ Production Environment Setup	5 days	Tue 11/26/02	Mon 12/2/02	17	0%	
32		⊟ Functional Testing	7 days	Tue 12/3/02	Wed 12/11/02	31	0%	
33		Status Meeting	1 day	Tue 12/3/02	Tue 12/3/02		0%	Project Manager
34	🔍	Execute Functional Test Plan	3 days	Tue 12/3/02	Thu 12/5/02		0%	Tester
35	🔍	Functional Testing Exception Document	1 day	Fri 12/6/02	Fri 12/6/02	34	0%	Tester
36		Functional Testing Corrections	3 days	Mon 12/9/02	Wed 12/11/02	35	0%	DBA,Developer
37		Functional Testing Sign-Off	0 days	Wed 12/11/02	Wed 12/11/02	36	0%	Stakeholders
38		⊟ Load Testing	3 days	Thu 12/12/02	Mon 12/16/02	32	0%	
39		Status Meeting	1 day	Thu 12/12/02	Thu 12/12/02		0%	Project Manager
40	🔍	Execute Load Test Plan	1 day	Thu 12/12/02	Thu 12/12/02		0%	DBA
41	🔍	Complete Load Testing Exception Document	1 day	Fri 12/13/02	Fri 12/13/02	40	0%	DBA
42		Load Testing Corrections	1 day	Mon 12/16/02	Mon 12/16/02	41	0%	DBA,Developer
43		Load Testing Sign-Off	0 days	Mon 12/16/02	Mon 12/16/02	42	0%	Stakeholders
44		⊟ End User Testing	5 days	Tue 12/17/02	Mon 12/23/02	38	0%	
45		Status Meeting	1 day	Tue 12/17/02	Tue 12/17/02		0%	Project Manager
46	🔍	Execute End User Test Plan	2 days	Tue 12/17/02	Wed 12/18/02		0%	Users
47	🔍	Complete End User Testing Exception Document	1 day	Thu 12/19/02	Thu 12/19/02	46	0%	Users
48		End User Testing Corrections	2 days	Fri 12/20/02	Mon 12/23/02	47	0%	DBA,Developer
49		End User Testing Sign-Off	0 days	Mon 12/23/02	Mon 12/23/02	48	0%	Stakeholders
50		⊞ User Training	7 days	Thu 12/12/02	Fri 12/20/02	32	0%	
54		⊞ SQL Server Upgrade	1 day	Tue 12/24/02	Tue 12/24/02	44	0%	
62		⊞ Lessons Learned	3 days	Wed 12/25/02	Fri 12/27/02	54	0%	

Figure 11.1: Project Plan — Functional, Load and End User Testing Tasks.

For the SQL Server 2000 Upgrade, the tasks shown in Figure 11.1 need to be addressed during the Functional, Load and End User Testing.

In order to minimize the level of effort for testing, it is essential to properly prepare for each test. This can be accomplished in a number of ways, from the overall test planning to the testing environment. It is also imperative to document the testing process to retest with subsequent changes and corrections. After the corrections, be prepared for a minimum of two testing cycles for retesting. Practically speaking, be prepared for an average of four rounds of testing.

Although there are numerous types of testing, I have found that two documents address the majority of the testing needs across all testing types to properly complete the testing phases. These documents are the Testing Plan and the Testing Exceptions document. These two basic documents serve as a framework that can be used to conduct the testing needed for most projects in an accurate and efficient manner.

Testing Plan

The Testing Plan, represented in Table 11.2 below, is a simple template to record the chronological testing sequence with sufficient detail to repeat the testing for subsequent test cycles. The reality is you have a test plan because problems will be encountered that need to be duplicated and subsequently corrected. Once these problems are corrected, it is necessary to retest in order to validate the entire testing sequence. With each one of these tests, a new Testing Plan should be created and frozen to record the steps and results for each test. This is absolutely necessary to compare results between the various testing cycles and ensure that the application is performing properly. The Testing Plan can be supplemented with testing scripts that will automate portions of the testing, and this can save valuable time in the long run. This may require a moderate amount of time to properly prepare meaningful and accurate scripts in the short term.

The Testing Plan records the individual test step, test step results, the Tester who is executing the individual step, the date completed, and subsequent comments. In most circumstances, this simple template can be modified to meet a variety of needs. The template can be extended at times, since multiple Testers may be responsible for a subset of the overall testing. It could be easily modularized by screen in the front end application or from an overall workflow with a corresponding Test Plan. Table 11.2 shows the Functional Testing Plan for the SQL Server 2000 Upgrade project.

SQL Server 6.5 to 2000 Upgrade – Functional Testing Plan					
ID	Test	Results	Tester	Date	Comments
1	Login to the application	Success	Laurie	12.03.2002	None
2	Main Screen – Search for a client	Success	Laurie	12.03.2002	Searched for John Smith
3	Main Screen – Update the Dummy record	Failure – Issues List	Laurie	12.03.2002	⊠ill speak with Dave
4	Main Screen – Insert a new Dummy record	Success	Laurie	12.03.2002	Add Dummy37
5	Vendor Screen – Request a Letter	Success	Laurie	12.03.2002	Requested Microsoft Bid
6	Vendor Screen – Search for Seattle Vendors	Success	Laurie	12.03.2002	25 Vendors Found
7	Employee Screen – Verify Call Total	Success	Laurie	12.03.2002	0 Calls
8	Out Going Call Screen – Place a Call	Failure – Issues List	Laurie	12.03.2002	⊠ill speak with Jim
9	Employee Screen – Verify Call Total	Success	Laurie	12.03.2002	1 Failure
10	In Coming Call Screen – Accept a Call	Success	Laurie	12.03.2002	Spoke with Jim
11	Employee Screen – Verify Call Total	Success	Laurie	12.03.2002	1 Failure & 1 Success
12	Partners Screen – Update a Partner	Success	Laurie	12.03.2002	Updated Compaq to HP-Compaq
13	Employee Screen – Generate Daily Activity Report	Success	Laurie	12.03.2002	Client, Vendor, Partner and Call Info
14	Employee Screen – Print Activity Report	Failure – Issues List	Laurie	12.03.2002	⊠ill speak with Jim
15	Log Out of Application	Failure – Issues List	Laurie	12.03.2002	Application hung on exit

Table 11.2: Core Project Document — Functional Testing Plan.

SQL Server 6.5 to 2000 Upgrade – Functional Testing Exceptions					
ID	Issue Information	Results		Date	Status
1	Main Screen – Update the Dummy record	Failure – Issues List	Laurie	12.03.2002	Open
	The Dummy record was not previously created in this database as is the case with test	Record Added – Requesting Re-Test	Dave	12.04.2002	Pending
	Re-Test with no problems	Success	Laurie	12.05.2002	Closed
2	Out Going Call Screen – Place A Call	Failure – Issues List	Laurie	12.03.2002	Open
	Reinstalled the CTI Integration App on the ⊠orkstation	Request Re-Test	Jim	12.05.2002	Pending
	Able to call outbound	Success	Laurie	12.06.2002	Closed
3	Employee Screen – Print Activity Report	Failure – Issues List	Laurie	12.03.2002	Open
	Suspect problem with Printer Drivers	Requesting Network Admins reinstall printer drivers	Jim	12.04.2002	Open
	Re-installed Printer Drivers and verified could print a test page	Re-Test	Joe	12.06.2002	Pending
	Re-tested printing	Success	Laurie	12.07.2002	Closed
4	Log Out of Application	Failure – Issues List	Laurie	12.03.2002	Open
	Re-tested per Jim's suggestion	Success	Laurie	12.04.2002	Closed

Table 11.3: Core Project Document — Functional Testing Exceptions Document.

Testing Exceptions

As shown in Table 11.3, the Testing Exceptions document compliments the Test Plan and is used to track failures from a particular Test Plan. There is a one-to-one ratio between the Test Plan and Testing Exceptions document. The Testing Exceptions document outlines the failures from the Test Plan. Then the Testing Exceptions document is used as a tool to track the corrections for all the problems encountered in the Test Plan. For example, the four failures shown on the Functional Testing Plan in Table 11.2 as IDs 3, 8, 14 and 15 correspond to IDs 1 to 4 on the Functional Testing Exceptions document shown in Table 11.3. The Testing Exceptions document should be used by the Testing and Development team members to correct the test problems that are ultimately overseen by the Project Manager. The status should also be regularly communicated and re-tested until unanimous success is achieved.

Testing Environment and Tools

In order to conduct proper and various types of testing, an appropriate test environment must be set up. The type of testing that is required dictates the test environment. If you are in an environment that does not have the luxury of a one-to-one ratio between Production, Test and Development environments, you may need to be a little creative. For example, during Functional Testing, a lower caliber set of hardware could be used to minimize costs as long as the production software is used. In this case, a PC could be used to merely verify that the application is performing properly. Unfortunately, this may not be the case when Load Testing is being conducted and it is necessary to stress test the application and related components. In this circumstance, if new hardware is being purchased, it may be advantageous to test with this equipment. If this is not the case, explore options such as leasing equipment for a few days or weeks from a hardware reseller to properly complete Load Testing. If you are not able to mimic the environment, the test results may be skewed, with the hardware causing the discrepancy.

Another area that has become a staple in many IT organizations is a suite of testing tools that address functional, load and integration testing needs. Many testing tools are available in the marketplace with a variety of functionality and associated costs. On one end of the spectrum is DBHammer from Microsoft, which is a free tool to load test SQL Server. On the other side of the spectrum is Mercury Interactive's Load Runner suite of testing tools for full scale testing across the entire application (see www.mercuryinteractive.com). I have also heard of organizations that have developed custom testing tools for streamlining the testing processes. Based on the testing needs, the appropriate tool must be available to trained staff for accurate and efficient completion of the project's testing requirements.

Lessons Learned

▶ Conduct the proper testing, such as Functional, User Acceptance, Load, Integration, etc., to verify that the application or process will operate as expected.

▶ Leverage a Testing Plan and Testing Exceptions document in order to properly conduct the necessary testing (Functional, User Acceptance, Load, Integration, etc.). Track the progression of corrections to properly complete the necessary testing.

▶ Establish and control a testing environment in conjunction with testing scripts and tools to streamline the testing process.

FREE

Bonus:

Sample Functional Testing documents are available as free downloads when you register your book at www.rationalpress.com.

Chapter 12

Training

"Let us train our minds to desire what the situation demands."
— *Lucius Annæus Seneca*

Unfortunately, training is one aspect of most projects that is typically overlooked and in some cases causes project failure. Do not contribute to this failure by neglecting to budget time and resources for user training. Whether the users are IT personnel or business users, ensure that an adequate amount of time is available for testing. Remember that if the users cannot use the application or follow the process, the project is a failure.

Training Options

Depending on the application and testing requirements a few training options may be available. Regardless of the type of training, your plan must allocate time and money to building a curriculum with training materials and to conduct effective training. The curriculum and training materials may vary dramatically, depending on the type of training. These items can range from a simple set of documents to a very complex set of training information in any of the settings shown in Table 12.1.

Training Options			
ID	Training Technique	Advantages	Disadvantages
1	One-on-one training	• Ability to take time to personalize the training and work at a pace that best suits the trainee • May generate the most productive users due to personal attention • Dedicated time to focus on training	• Can be very costly and time-consuming to train individual users
2	Traditional classroom training led by a Trainer (small to mid sized groups)	• Ideal when trying to teach a business critical application to the entire user community • Ability to ask questions and some personal attention on a small scale • Dedicated time to focus on training	• Need to have training facilities to accommodate the entire group • Need to ensure no one breezes by the training and does not get overlooked
3	Online self-paced training	• Self-paced nature permits users to learn at their own pace	• No opportunity for personal attention or to address questions • Users must be computer savvy in order to complete the training
4	Teach a base group of trainers and this group teaches the remainder of the users	• Efficient way to teach a base group of users such as power users or front line managers and have them spread the word	• Message may be lost in the relay • Some lessons may be open to misinterpretations • The base group would need to have the skills to train other users
5	Build and distribute application cheat sheets or a user guide	• Self-paced nature permits users to learn at their own pace • Point of reference for future usage with the application • May work well in conjunction with other training methods	• A non-motivated user may not take the time to learn the application • May lend itself to a situation where the users do not accept the application
6	Group works with a Trainer	• Has the ability to leverage ideas from multiple team members to solve the problem • Ideal for situations when the entire team must be able to work together to solve the problem • Has the benefit of the trainer to structure the seminar	• May not be the most efficient short term solution to convey the important training information
7	Divide, conquer and train the group	• Each member of the training group is responsible for learning a portion of the curriculum and teaches the remainder of the group • Old adage is that you really do not know something unless you can explain it yourself	• Could be time consuming and individual users may need assistance from a trainer in order to deliver the correct message

Table 12.1: Training Phase — Training Option Analysis.

Often, combinations of these techniques are used in unison to achieve a well-trained staff. If you are responsible for developing a training curriculum, do not be afraid to mix and match options to teach particular portions of the application. Please keep in mind that people learn in one of the three ways outlined in Chapter 5: 1) visual (seeing), 2) verbal (hearing) or 3) kinesthetic (doing). Therefore, if a single approach is used, two-thirds of the users may not be learning in the most efficient manner. This concept becomes important when critical aspects of the application or process must be conveyed.

As the Project Manager, make sure that the most appropriate type and amount of training is being offered. If this is not the case, raise the issue to ensure that the users are properly trained. The fact remains that insufficient training does not yield a productive work force and can cause failure.

Insufficient training is one problem I fell victim to on a recent project I was managing. I was responsible for training a group of Project Managers and users to complete a series of similar projects. Training was in the overall Project Scope and Project Plan, but the Stakeholders pushed the envelope too hard and training was quickly lost. The Stakeholders ended up with a staff that was not trained, but expected to read the documentation and perform the tasks. Luckily, they were able to do so in most circumstances. But in a few situations, the users did not take the time to read the documentation and quickly became frustrated with results that fell short of their expectations. It required additional time from me on a one-on-one basis to get them on track and change their negative perceptions to positive ones.

In this situation, the problem could have been easily resolved with half a day of training for the entire team. The prepared documentation served as the user guide for the project and was leveraged after the training, but was no substitute for actual training. The base group could have trained the new team members based on their original training and subsequent project experiences.

Although each of the strategies listed in Figure 12.1 can yield success, I observed a new approach by a very progressive company. This company tested the users on their accuracy and efficiency in using the application. Based on the testing scores, a financial reward was given to the most accurate and efficient users.

Needless to say, all of the users worked diligently for this reward on a regular basis and continuously sought to improve the application in order to win the financial reward.

In the SQL Server 2000 Project, a finite number of users are involved, and the Project Team is responsible for the Upgrade. Small group training would be the best approach. Figure 12.1 outlines the SQL Server 2000 Training Tasks for the IT staff.

	0	Task Name	Duration	Start	Finish	Prede	% omplet	Resource Names
1		⊟ SQL Server 6.5 to 2000 Upgrade	40 days	Mon 11/4/02	Fri 12/27/02		0%	
2		⊞ Project Scope	4 days	Mon 11/4/02	Thu 11/7/02		0%	
9		⊞ Requirements Analysis	7 days	Fri 11/8/02	Mon 11/18/02	2	0%	
17		⊞ Test Environment Setup	5 days	Tue 11/19/02	Mon 11/25/02	9	0%	
21		⊞ Preliminary Upgrade Testing	5 days	Tue 11/26/02	Mon 12/2/02	17	0%	
28		⊞ Production Environment Setup	5 days	Tue 11/26/02	Mon 12/2/02	17	0%	
32		⊞ Functional Testing	7 days	Tue 12/3/02	Wed 12/11/02	31	0%	
38		⊞ Load Testing	3 days	Thu 12/12/02	Mon 12/16/02	32	0%	
44		⊞ End User Testing	5 days	Tue 12/17/02	Mon 12/23/02	38	0%	
50		⊟ User Training	7 days	Thu 12/12/02	Fri 12/20/02	32	0%	
51	📖	Write Training Curriculum	5 days	Thu 12/12/02	Wed 12/18/02		0%	Trainer
52	📖	Train and Test Users	2 days	Thu 12/19/02	Fri 12/20/02	51	0%	Users,Trainer
53	📖	User Training Sign-Off	0 days	Fri 12/20/02	Fri 12/20/02	52	0%	Stakeholders
54		⊞ SQL Server Upgrade	1 day	Tue 12/24/02	Tue 12/24/02	44	0%	

Figure 12.1: Project Plan — User Training Project Plan Tasks.

Lessons Learned

▶ Determine the most appropriate means to teach the user community and devise a strategy for the users to achieve optimal productivity with the application.

▶ Ensure that the appropriate type and amount of training is provided for users. This will prevent frustration and enable the users to properly leverage the application or process.

Chapter 13

Implementation

"When things are difficult, remember if it wasn't difficult everyone would be doing it. Difficulties are what makes us great."
— *Dan Brent Burt*

You have made it to the implementation door step. Now is the time when the "rubber meets the road" and you need to make use of all the Design, Development and Testing lessons learned thus far to ensure a successfully implemented project. The Implementation phase consists of the GO/NO GO Meeting, the Implementation and Release to Production. These steps are outlined for the SQL Server 2000 Upgrade Implementation in Figure 13.1, which also includes Pre-Upgrade and Post-Upgrade code releases.

	o	Task Name	Duration	Start	Finish	Prede	% Complete	Resource Names
1		⊟ SQL Server 6.5 to 2000 Upgrade	40 days	Mon 11/4/02	Fri 12/27/02		0%	
2		⊞ Project Scope	4 days	Mon 11/4/02	Thu 11/7/02		0%	
9		⊞ Requirements Analysis	7 days	Fri 11/8/02	Mon 11/18/02	2	0%	
17		⊞ Test Environment Setup	5 days	Tue 11/19/02	Mon 11/25/02	9	0%	
21		⊞ Preliminary Upgrade Testing	5 days	Tue 11/26/02	Mon 12/2/02	17	0%	
28		⊞ Production Environment Setup	6 days	Tue 11/26/02	Mon 12/2/02	17	0%	
32		⊞ Functional Testing	7 days	Tue 12/3/02	Wed 12/11/02	31	0%	
38		⊞ Load Testing	3 days	Thu 12/12/02	Mon 12/16/02	32	0%	
44		⊞ End User Testing	5 days	Tue 12/17/02	Mon 12/23/02	38	0%	
50		⊞ User Training	7 days	Thu 12/12/02	Fri 12/20/02	32	0%	
54		⊟ SQL Server Upgrade	1 day	Tue 12/24/02	Tue 12/24/02	44	0%	
55		Go	No Go Meeting	1 day	Tue 12/24/02	Tue 12/24/02		0%	Project Manager
56	⊞ ✎	⊟ SQL Server 6.5 to 2000 Upgrade	1 day	Tue 12/24/02	Tue 12/24/02		0%	
57		Apply Pre-Upgrade Code	1 day	Tue 12/24/02	Tue 12/24/02		0%	DBA
58		SQL Server 6.5 to 2000 Upgrade	1 day	Tue 12/24/02	Tue 12/24/02		0%	DBA
59		Apply Post-Upgrade Code	1 day	Tue 12/24/02	Tue 12/24/02		0%	DBA
60		Post Upgrade Testing	1 day	Tue 12/24/02	Tue 12/24/02		0%	Tester,Users
61		Certify the SQL Server 6.5 to 2000 Upgrade	0 days	Tue 12/24/02	Tue 12/24/02	60	0%	DBA,Stakeholders
62		⊞ Lessons Learned	3 days	Wed 12/25/02	Fri 12/27/02	54	0%	

Figure 13.1: Project Plan — SQL Server Upgrade Implementation Project Plan Tasks.

GO/NO GO Meeting

The final step before the actual implementation of the project is the GO/NO GO meeting. This meeting is intended to serve as a final checkpoint prior to the implementation, where all issues are brought to the table one last time. All open items on the Issues List should be assessed as to whether they are irresolvable and significant enough to prevent the project from moving forward as scheduled.

At this point, there should be no surprises. Ideally, you should have no issues remaining and if issues still exist on the Issues List, everyone should be well aware of them and the required course of action to be taken. In addition, you should ask if any new issues should be addressed prior to the implementation. Review any contingency plans that have been created, and the overall escalation procedures. Conclude the meeting with a GO or NO GO vote from everyone on the team. If a GO vote is reached, proceed to the implementation. If a NO GO vote is cast, systematically address the items and ensure consensus among the team or institute a contingency plan to meet the project deadlines.

If everything goes as planned, this 15 to 30 minute meeting between all of the Implementation Staff and Stakeholders should yield a consensus to move forward with the implementation (GO). Once the consensus is reached, an entry in the Change Management Process should be issued. Send the Sign-Off to the Stakeholders and obtain written agreement from all Stakeholders to formally proceed with the implementation. Remember, the written agreement can be obtained using emails as outlined in the "Project Phase Sign-Offs" section of Chapter 5.

I cannot overemphasize the importance of the GO/NO GO meeting as the first critical component of the implementation phase. Do not make the mistake of not having proper group representation and overlooking a team member that is not in agreement with the team's decision. Do not pressure anyone to make a decision. It may come back to haunt you, considering the level of effort that will be needed to complete the implementation.

Furthermore, if problems do exist, do not be afraid to prevent the upgrade from proceeding. Determine how to resolve the problems to cut your losses in an expedited manner. Be careful of a team member who says problems are "no big deal." Typically, this assessment is a simplification and the items should have been addressed earlier in the project. If the problem existed during the Design, Development or Testing phase and was not addressed, it must be resolved and the project should not proceed. Most problems are not simple and if they were, they would have simple answers and not be an issue prior to implementation.

Finally, depending on the length of the implementation, incorporate checkpoints to communicate the overall status. For example, if you are upgrading a 100+ GB database from SQL Server 6.5 to SQL Server 2000, 24+ hours may be needed. In order for the testing staff to be available, notify the team on a four to five hour basis of the status to ease everyone's nerves and properly set expectations.

Implementation: SQL Server 2000 Upgrade

Prior to starting the implementation, ensure that the following items have been completed:

▶ A Change Management entry has been submitted, communicated and approved.

▶ Verify that a GO decision from the GO/NO GO meeting has been reached.

▶ Confirm that Sign-Off approvals from all Stakeholders have been received by the Project Manager.

If you are on the implementation staff, review the appropriate documentation one last time to begin working in Execution Mode for the implementation. This phase is not for making decisions, but for walking through the exact steps prescribed to successfully complete the implementation.

Use the Implementation Plan created during the Design, Development and Testing phase as your step-by-step guide. I recommend adding a column to the Implementation Plan called "Status" to record the general success or failure, as well as the detailed output or a Hyperlink to the screen shot or text file. In addition, print out the Implementation Plan, especially if you need to work behind the server console in a loud server room. As you proceed, check off each step and record the needed output to have a complete record of all of the inputs and outputs during the process.

When the implementation begins, work through the SQL Server 2000 Upgrade Checklist step by step. As you go through the process, be sure to measure twice and cut once. If the wrong option is selected or the incorrect code is applied, the rework can be time-consuming and cause major delays. To combat this problem, use the "2 Man Rule," which is to have two sets of eyes review the process and selections. Have one person make the selections and a second person be responsible for observing and validating the selections, code and process. A good team can quickly and accurately complete the process without a flaw.

As portions of the process are being completed, review the output to make sure it is accurate and expected. If you encounter a problem that is not expected or a general error, record all of the information and take screen shots to troubleshoot and clearly communicate. Repeat the steps to verify that a mistake was not made by accident. If you are unable to correct the problem, escalate the issue to have the remainder of the team address it, or gather the proper information to return to the Design, Development and Testing phase. The severity of the problem should dictate a needed course of action: to correct the oversight and continue with the implementation, or return to earlier stages of the project and complete the implementation at a later date.

When you are able to complete the process without any errors and are personally satisfied with the results, notify the Testing team that the implementation is completed and request Pre-Release testing. The Pre-Release testing should be the execution of the Functional Test Plan. Compare the results from the Pre-Release testing to the previously conducted Functional Testing (performed during the Formalized Testing phase earlier in the project). These results should be compared to validate that the outcome does not have any discrepancies and the application is performing properly prior to releasing it to the users. Also, depending on the application, it may be advantageous to have a user conduct the End User Test Plan to gain his or her overall support for the platform. It could also be advantageous to successfully test on a few different PC's.

Once the Testing team and the Users have concluded that the application is performing properly and validated it as a successful upgrade, notify the remainder of the team of the status. Hold an informal meeting with the team to make sure all t's are crossed and i's are dotted. Seek agreement from the entire team to proceed with the Release to Production steps. Attain overall agreement to certify the Upgrade from SQL Server 6.5 to 2000 and move to the Release to Production phase.

Release to Production

Once the implementation has been certified, make any necessary final configuration changes to release the platform to the production environment. This final release should also include updating the remainder of the client PCs. Upon completion, notify the users that the application is available and that they should discontinue the use of the previous application. Also, update the Change Management process to reflect the successful implementation. Finally, check in with the users or Help Desk on a regular basis for at least one week following the implementation to ensure that the application is not experiencing any problems.

Lessons Learned

▶ Conduct a GO/NO GO Meeting to make sure the team is prepared and in agreement to move forward.

▶ Operate in Execution Mode during the Implementation. Follow a checklist instead of making last-minute decisions. Leverage the "2 Man Rule" to have a team members to work in tandem for the implementation.

▶ After the Implementation, test again to certify the Upgrade and release to the users.

Chapter 14

Lessons Learned

"It's not enough to be good if you have the ability to be better."
— Alberta Lee Cox

You have finally made it through the SQL Server 2000 Upgrade. Congratulations on your success! Now you, your team and your company are reaping the benefits of all of your blood, sweat and tears. Although the Upgrade is completed, the project is still not over. It is time to assemble the entire team one last time for a project wrap up and discussion.

This final meeting is intended to wrap up the project and to determine the Lessons Learned during the project, in order to benefit future projects. The tasks associated with this phase for the SQL Server 2000 Project are outlined in Figure 14.1. Although the list is short, it is critical in determining how to improve future projects.

	O	Task Name	Duration	Start	Finish	Prede	% Complete	Resource Names
1		⊟ SQL Server 6.5 to 2000 Upgrade	40 days	Mon 11/4/02	Fri 12/27/02		0%	
2		⊞ Project Scope	4 days	Mon 11/4/02	Thu 11/7/02		0%	
9		⊞ Requirements Analysis	7 days	Fri 11/8/02	Mon 11/18/02	2	0%	
17		⊞ Test Environment Setup	5 days	Tue 11/19/02	Mon 11/25/02	9	0%	
21		⊞ Preliminary Upgrade Testing	5 days	Tue 11/26/02	Mon 12/2/02	17	0%	
28		⊞ Production Environment Setup	5 days	Tue 11/26/02	Mon 12/2/02	17	0%	
32		⊞ Functional Testing	7 days	Tue 12/3/02	Wed 12/11/02	31	0%	
36		⊞ Load Testing	3 days	Thu 12/12/02	Mon 12/16/02	32	0%	
44		⊞ End User Testing	5 days	Tue 12/17/02	Mon 12/23/02	36	0%	
50		⊞ User Training	7 days	Thu 12/12/02	Fri 12/20/02	32	0%	
54		⊞ SQL Server Upgrade	1 day	Tue 12/24/02	Tue 12/24/02	44	0%	
62		⊟ Lessons Learned	3 days	Wed 12/25/02	Fri 12/27/02	64	0%	
63		Lessons Learned Meeting	1 day	Wed 12/25/02	Wed 12/25/02		0%	Project Manager
64	🗓	Project Completion Survey	1 day	Thu 12/26/02	Thu 12/26/02	63	0%	All Staff
65	🗓	Determine Lessons Learned	1 day	Fri 12/27/02	Fri 12/27/02	64	0%	Project Manager

Figure 14.1: Project Plan — Lessons Learned Project Plan Tasks.

It is imperative to determine the project successes and failures via constructive feedback from the team at the Lessons Learned meeting. As the Project Manager, ensure that the comments are professional and are not personal attacks against any of the team members. Once this information is provided in the Lessons Learned meeting, inform the team that you are going to distribute a Lessons Learned Survey to obtain anonymous feedback from the group with the intention of improving future projects.

In the meeting, do not be afraid to probe for information from the team members. It may be a good idea to talk about some of your personal Lessons Learned and then ask for feedback. See if anyone on the team can think of other ways to complete the tasks in a more efficient manner. It may also be advantageous to talk about the project on a per phase basis and identify the Lessons Learned at that level. The bottom line is to determine how to operate in a more efficient and accurate manner for the next project.

Before the conclusion of the meeting, take the time to sincerely thank everyone on the team for their efforts on the project. I recommend having a happy hour or team lunch to celebrate the success of the project. If you have made significant improvements, see if the organization is willing to foot the bill for this small party. If you have done your due diligence with the Cost Benefit Analysis (and the Stakeholders can see the benefit in dollars and cents), they will usually support this type of celebration. To take it a step further, recognize individuals on the team for their contributions to the success of the project. End on a positive note and prepare for the next project!

Lessons Learned Survey

Table 14.1 offers a baseline Lessons Learned Survey that can easily be modified for a variety of projects to obtain valuable feedback. This survey has a balance of both quantifiable and qualitative questions to gather the necessary information. The reality is that although you ask for feedback among the team members, sometimes you do not get the complete picture. The anonymous survey allows the entire team to express their feelings. People are generally more open in this anonymous atmosphere and provide more information.

Immediately after the meeting, distribute the Lessons Learned Survey to obtain feedback. Once you have obtained all of the Lessons Learned Surveys, analyze the results to determine a succinct set of Lessons Learned. These items can be the areas where future projects can be improved upon or items that were completed properly that need to be consistent for future projects. Once the Lessons Learned are compiled, distribute this information to benefit the team. It may also be beneficial to share the knowledge with other groups, so they can derive benefits for future projects.

As the Project Manager, you can also use this as a tool to rate your personal effectiveness and the effectiveness of the Project Management process that was leveraged to complete the project. Take the time use the feedback to determine ways to improve future projects. You will often obtain feedback that can guide your future projects, or techniques to work with individuals to improve the overall Communication Plan. Finally, the Lessons Learned Surveys could also be used during evaluations for raises or references for future projects.

SQL Server 6.5 to 2000 Upgrade – Lessons Learned Survey		

INSTRUCTIONS
- Rate the recent project according to the questions below.
- Return to the Project Manager by 12.26.2002 in an anonymous manner.
- All results will be shared following the Lessons Learned Meeting.
- Lessons Learned Survey Ratings are 1 to 10 with:

    1– Low   **5– Average**   **10 – High**

ID	QUESTION	RATING	ADDITIONAL COMMENTS
1	How would you rate the overall project?		
2	How would you rate the project leadership?		
3	How would you rate your understanding of your expectations?		
4	How would you rate the task timeline?		
5	How would you rate the project web site?		
6	How would you rate the communication?		
7	How would you rate the documentation?		
8	How could future projects be improved?	N/A	
9	⊠hat do you think was the worst portion of the project? How can this be corrected?	N/A	
10	⊠hat are your additional comments?	N/A	

Table14.1: Core Project Document — Lessons Learned Survey.

Lessons Learned

▶ Determine project successes and failures by completing the Lessons Learned phase. This phase is essential to and will benefit future projects.

▶ Make sure to share these lessons among the team and organization.

▶ In order to improve future projects, obtain feedback not only from the Lessons Learned meeting, but also from the anonymous Lessons Learned Survey.

▶ Celebrate the team's success and take the opportunity to spotlight the contributions to the project.

Chapter 15

Conclusion

"Determination, hard work and persistence cannot be underestimated in achieving success!"
— Jeremy Kadlec

Project Management is the application of a comprehensive process directed by a highly skilled Project Manager in the form of a definable project to benefit an organization by achieving the project goals. In light of numerous Project Management challenges, the techniques discussed in this book and summarized below will yield project success:

▶ Streamline the Project Management process to manage the implementation of a successful solution. Define, Organize, Document, Communicate and Manage.

▶ Create a comprehensive Project Plan with accurate Resources, Dependencies and Durations at the appropriate level of detail.

▶ Assemble a cohesive team with excited Team Members and committed Stakeholders.

▶ Assemble talented Team Members who are experts in their respective field(s).

▶ Create a Communication Plan with open communication, regularly scheduled meetings and centralized project information accessible to the entire team for updates.

► Create beneficial documentation to support the project and historical needs.

► Commit to risk mitigation, option analysis for the ideal course of action, and the quick closing of Issues List items.

► Schedule productive Status Meetings for team contributions and overall goal achievement.

► Create an understandable Project Scope with tangible goals and an agreed-upon Requirements Analysis for the team to strive to exceed on a daily basis.

► Create solid Design, Development and Baseline Testing for the application or process.

► Recognize and prevent curve balls that might endanger the project.

► Establish a Testing environment and Testing Plan to verify the functionality of the application or process in your environment and under significant load.

► Implement appropriate training.

► Ensure timely Sign-Off on all phases of the Project from Stakeholders.

► Adhere to all project phase deadlines to remain on-schedule and within budget.

► Successfully use people, processes and technology that will benefit the organization, fulfill the organizational needs and meet the project goals.

I cannot overemphasize the value that I have gained from numerous projects in my career that I have shared as my experiences in this book. I am especially grateful for the numerous items brought forward from the Lessons Learned meetings and Surveys. Many of the items listed in this publication are from feedback gathered in the Lessons Learned meetings, as well as time I have taken for self-assessment to determine how to improve my personal effectiveness as a Project Manager. One of the best examples is the Communication Plan described in Chapter 5, as well as the "Working with Difficult Team Members" section in Chapter 8. Both items are derived from lessons that I have learned from a number of different projects and people. I hope these items will benefit you.

I would like to share one last item regarding the writing of this book. I approached it as a project with the process outlined in Chapter 1 and a consolidated list of documents. I leveraged many of the applicable techniques outlined in many of the chapters for proper planning and decision making to meet the deadlines. These techniques proved valuable even with a small team that relied on one primary resource. The same should be true for you at your organization when addressing critical projects. You can leverage these techniques on a team of one, a small departmental team or a large enterprise team. Needless to say, I will continue to practice these techniques and generate new ones, because I am certain that with each project I will be able to fine tune my skills for greater improvements.

I hope this publication has been beneficial to you and I wish you great success on your future projects. Good luck!

Bonus:

The following items are available as free downloads when you register your book at `www.rationalpress.com`.

► Sample documents for use in your own projects, including Sample SQL Server 6.5 to SQL Server 2000 Upgrade project file, Cost Benefit Analysis, Feasibility Analysis, Meeting Agenda Minutes, Requirements Analysis, and more

► Sample email communications between project team members

► Bonus chapters: "Taking Over a Project Gone Wrong" and "Maintenance"

Part IV

Extras

Appendix A

Sample Project Plan

"Success is good management in action."
— William E. Holler

Throughout the book, snippets of the SQL Server 2000 Project Plan have been included to visualize the tasks associated with a particular phase. The complete Project Plan that served as an example project throughout the book is shown on the next page.

	o	Task Name	Duration	Start	Finish	Prede	% omplet	Resource Names
1		⊟ SQL Server 6.5 to 2000 Upgrade	40 days	Mon 11/4/02	Fri 12/27/02		0%	
2		⊟ Project Scope	4 days	Mon 11/4/02	Thu 11/7/02		0%	
3		Project Scope Meeting	1 day	Mon 11/4/02	Mon 11/4/02		0%	Project Manager
4		Determine Key Staff, Stakeholders, Budget and Goals	1 day	Mon 11/4/02	Mon 11/4/02		0%	Project Manager
5		Compile the Feasibility Analysis	1 day	Tue 11/5/02	Tue 11/5/02	4	0%	Project Manager
6		Calculate the Cost Benefit Analysis	1 day	Wed 11/6/02	Wed 11/6/02	5	0%	Project Manager
7		Project Scope Review and Editing	1 day	Thu 11/7/02	Thu 11/7/02	6	0%	Project Manager,Stakeholders
8		Project Scope Sign-Off	0 days	Thu 11/7/02	Thu 11/7/02	7	0%	Stakeholders
9		⊟ Requirements Analysis	7 days	Fri 11/8/02	Mon 11/18/02	2	0%	
10		Kick Off Meeting	1 day	Fri 11/8/02	Fri 11/8/02		0%	Project Manager
11		Identify, Order and Obtain Hardware	7 days	Fri 11/8/02	Mon 11/18/02		0%	Network Admin
12		Develop Test Plans	7 days	Fri 11/8/02	Mon 11/18/02		0%	Tester
13		SQL Server Configurations and Security	7 days	Fri 11/8/02	Mon 11/18/02		0%	DBA
14		Determine Communication Procedure	1 day	Fri 11/8/02	Fri 11/8/02		0%	Project Manager
15		Complete Requirements Analysis	7 days	Fri 11/8/02	Mon 11/18/02		0%	Project Manager
16		Requirements Analysis Sign-Off	0 days	Mon 11/18/02	Mon 11/18/02	15	0%	Stakeholders
17		⊟ Test Environment Setup	5 days	Tue 11/19/02	Mon 11/25/02	9	0%	
18		Status Meeting	1 day	Tue 11/19/02	Tue 11/19/02		0%	Project Manager
19		Setup Hardware	5 days	Tue 11/19/02	Mon 11/25/02		0%	Network Admin,DBA,Tester
20		Test Environment Sign-Off	0 days	Mon 11/25/02	Mon 11/25/02	19	0%	Stakeholders
21		⊟ Preliminary Upgrade Testing	5 days	Tue 11/26/02	Mon 12/2/02	17	0%	
22		Status Meeting	1 day	Tue 11/26/02	Tue 11/26/02		0%	Project Manager
23		Design and Develop Upgrade Process	2 days	Tue 11/26/02	Wed 11/27/02		0%	DBA
24		Test Upgrade Process and Finalize Documentation	1 day	Thu 11/28/02	Thu 11/28/02	23	0%	DBA
25		Execute Preliminary Upgrade	1 day	Fri 11/29/02	Fri 11/29/02	24	0%	DBA
26		Preliminary Upgrade Exceptions Document	1 day	Mon 12/2/02	Mon 12/2/02	25	0%	DBA
27		Preliminary Upgrade Sign-Off	0 days	Mon 12/2/02	Mon 12/2/02	26	0%	Stakeholders
28		⊟ Production Environment Setup	5 days	Tue 11/26/02	Mon 12/2/02	17	0%	
29		Status Meeting	1 day	Tue 11/26/02	Tue 11/26/02		0%	Project Manager
30		Setup Hardware	5 days	Tue 11/26/02	Mon 12/2/02		0%	Network Admin,DBA
31		Production Environment Sign-Off	0 days	Mon 12/2/02	Mon 12/2/02	30	0%	Stakeholders
32		⊟ Functional Testing	7 days	Tue 12/3/02	Wed 12/11/02	31	0%	
33		Status Meeting	1 day	Tue 12/3/02	Tue 12/3/02		0%	Project Manager
34		Execute Functional Test Plan	3 days	Tue 12/3/02	Thu 12/5/02		0%	Tester
35		Functional Testing Exception Document	1 day	Fri 12/6/02	Fri 12/6/02	34	0%	Tester
36		Functional Testing Corrections	3 days	Mon 12/9/02	Wed 12/11/02	35	0%	DBA,Developer
37		Functional Testing Sign-Off	0 days	Wed 12/11/02	Wed 12/11/02	36	0%	Stakeholders
38		⊟ Load Testing	3 days	Thu 12/12/02	Mon 12/16/02	32	0%	
39		Status Meeting	1 day	Thu 12/12/02	Thu 12/12/02		0%	Project Manager
40		Execute Load Test Plan	1 day	Thu 12/12/02	Thu 12/12/02		0%	DBA
41		Complete Load Testing Exception Document	1 day	Fri 12/13/02	Fri 12/13/02	40	0%	DBA
42		Load Testing Corrections	1 day	Mon 12/16/02	Mon 12/16/02	41	0%	DBA,Developer
43		Load Testing Sign-Off	0 days	Mon 12/16/02	Mon 12/16/02	42	0%	Stakeholders

		Task Name	Duration	Start	Finish	Prede	%	Resource Names
44		⊟ End User Testing	5 days	Tue 12/17/02	Mon 12/23/02	38	0%	
45		Status Meeting	1 day	Tue 12/17/02	Tue 12/17/02		0%	Project Manager
46		Execute End User Test Plan	2 days	Tue 12/17/02	Wed 12/18/02		0%	Users
47		Complete End User Testing Exception Document	1 day	Thu 12/19/02	Thu 12/19/02	46	0%	Users
48		End User Testing Corrections	2 days	Fri 12/20/02	Mon 12/23/02	47	0%	DBA,Developer
49		End User Testing Sign-Off	0 days	Mon 12/23/02	Mon 12/23/02	48	0%	Stakeholders
50		⊟ User Training	7 days	Thu 12/12/02	Fri 12/20/02	32	0%	
51		Write Training Curriculum	5 days	Thu 12/12/02	Wed 12/18/02		0%	Trainer
52		Train and Test Users	2 days	Thu 12/19/02	Fri 12/20/02	51	0%	Users,Trainer
53		User Training Sign-Off	0 days	Fri 12/20/02	Fri 12/20/02	52	0%	Stakeholders
54		⊟ SQL Server Upgrade	1 day	Tue 12/24/02	Tue 12/24/02	44	0%	
55		Go	No Go Meeting	1 day	Tue 12/24/02	Tue 12/24/02		0%	Project Manager
56		⊟ SQL Server 6.5 to 2000 Upgrade	1 day	Tue 12/24/02	Tue 12/24/02		0%	
57		Apply Pre-Upgrade Code	1 day	Tue 12/24/02	Tue 12/24/02		0%	DBA
58		SQL Server 6.5 to 2000 Upgrade	1 day	Tue 12/24/02	Tue 12/24/02		0%	DBA
59		Apply Post-Upgrade Code	1 day	Tue 12/24/02	Tue 12/24/02		0%	DBA
60		Post Upgrade Testing	1 day	Tue 12/24/02	Tue 12/24/02		0%	Tester,Users
61		Certify the SQL Server 6.5 to 2000 Upgrade	0 days	Tue 12/24/02	Tue 12/24/02	60	0%	DBA,Stakeholders
62		⊟ Lessons Learned	3 days	Wed 12/25/02	Fri 12/27/02	54	0%	
63		Lessons Learned Meeting	1 day	Wed 12/25/02	Wed 12/25/02		0%	Project Manager
64		Project Completion Survey	1 day	Thu 12/26/02	Thu 12/26/02	63	0%	All Staff
65		Determine Lessons Learned	1 day	Fri 12/27/02	Fri 12/27/02	64	0%	Project Manager

Notes

IMPORTANT NOTICE
REGISTER YOUR BOOK

Bonus Materials

Your book refers to valuable material that complements your learning experience. In order to download these materials you will need to register your book at http://www.rationalpress.com.

This bonus material is available after registration:

- ▶ Sample documents for use in your own projects, including Sample SQL Server 6.5 to SQL Server 2000 Upgrade project file, Cost Benefit Analysis, Feasibility Analysis, Meeting Agenda Minutes, and Requirements Analysis

- ▶ Sample email communications between project team members

- ▶ Bonus chapters: "Taking Over a Project Gone Wrong" and "Maintenance"

Registering your book

To register your book follow these 7 easy steps:

1. Go to http://www.rationalpress.com.
2. Create an account and login.
3. Click the **My Books** link.
4. Click the **Register New Book** button.
5. Enter the registration number found on the back of the book (Figure A).
6. Confirm registration and view your new book on the virtual bookshelf.
7. Click the spine of the desired book to view the available downloads and resources for the selected book.

Figure A: Back of your book.